THE

EASY

QUIZ

MASTER

Questions and Answers for a *Whole Year's worth* of Quiz Nights

By PETER ALLEN

LUCKY COOL PUBLICATIONS 2008

INDEX

Welcome Quizmasters and Quiz Enthusiasts alike. This book is intended to provide you with enough Quiz Questions, arranged in rounds, so that you can run a Quiz Night once a week throughout the year. We've taken the hassle out of preparing quiz questions EVERY WEEK so that you can concentrate on the fun aspects of running your Quiz Nights.

Even if you only run a Quiz Night occasionally, this book gives you the opportunity to have ready made questions, which you can trust, to entertain and inform your audience.

These questions are 'tried and tested' and are of a sufficient level that most teams will get at least half of them right, making for a more enjoyable evening for all.

Each quiz starts with a "Pot Luck" round and finishes with "Take A Chance" which gives teams a chance to make up lost ground...or to end up even further behind!!

If five rounds of questions per quiz are not enough, we would suggest putting together a music round and/or a picture round to vary the content for your audience.

Some months have five chances for a Quiz Night and to take account of this there are four sets of Bonus questions to be found at the back of this book.

Peter Allen has presented Pub Quiz Nights for the last seven years, so he knows what you are going through...and this book is the answer to your problems.

JANUARY

POT LUCK 01

1. Which long running radio programme was first broadcast on 1st January 1951?

2. Which Prime Minister introduced the poll Tax?

3. Who became the youngest person to write his own No. 1 hit when "Fill Me In" topped the UK charts in 2000?

4. In which country is the Natal National Park?

5. Cataracts affect which part of the body?

6. In Greek mythology, which creature was half man and half bull?

7. Who wrote "The Rime of the Ancient Mariner"?

8. Which monarch was beheaded in Whitehall in 1649?

9. In which sport is a shuttlecock used?

10. Ska music was developed in which country?

ANSWERS:

1. "The Archers"

2. Margaret Thatcher

3. Craig David

4. South Africa

5. Eyes

6. Minotaur

7. Samuel Taylor Coleridge

8. Charles I

9. Badminton

10. Jamaica

EUROPE

1. The River Elbe flows into which sea?

2. In which country is the port of Cadiz?

3. What is the largest city in Holland?

4. Which city is served by Charles de Gaulle Airport?

5. The Carbonari was a secret society in which country?

6. What is the currency of Liechtenstein?

7. The kings of Norway are crowned in the cathedral of which fishing port?

8. The Eiger is situated in which mountain range?

9. Cologne strands on which river?

10. The River Danube flows into which sea?

ANSWERS:

1. North Sea

2. Spain

3. Amsterdam

4. Paris

5. Italy

6. Swiss Franc

7. Trondheim

8. Alps

9. Rhine

10. Black Sea

THE TOP TEN

1. Who directed the 1934 film "It Happened One Night"?

2. Who wrote the novel "A Tale of Two Cities"?

3. Which is the only horse to have won the Grand National three times?

4. Whose 1986 recording of Vivaldi's "The Four Seasons" sold over 1 million copies?

5. Which striker scored five hat-tricks in the 1995-96 FA Carling Premiership?

6. Which country did Italy beat in their first ever Six Nations Rugby match?

7. Which of the seven dwarfs wore spectacles?

8. Which film won eight Oscars in 1982?

9. Who wrote the novel "The Nine Tailors" which featured the detective Lord Peter Wimsey?

10. Who played Moses in the 1956 film "The Ten Commandments"?

ANSWERS:

1. Frank Capra

2. Charles Dickens

3. Red Rum

4. Nigel Kennedy

5. Alan Shearer

6. Scotland

7. Doc

8. "Gandhi"

9. Dorothy L Sayers

10. Charlton Heston

CONNECTION

1. Which actor played Perry Mason on TV from 1957 to 1966 and from 1985 to 1993?

2. Which female singer had a top 5 hit with "I'm Like a Bird" in 2001?

3. Who played the title role in the film "Wayne's World"?

4. Which ice hockey player was known as 'The Great One'?

5. Which actress played CJ Parker in "Baywatch"?

6. Who directed the 1997 film "Titanic"?

7. Which singer won the Eurovision Song Contest representing Switzerland in 1988?

8. Which player won the World Professional Snooker title in 1980?

9. Who played 'Scotty' in "Star Trek"?

10. What is the connection between these people?

ANSWERS:

1. Raymond Burr

2. Nelly Furtado

3. Mike Myers

4. Wayne Gretsky

5. Pamela Anderson

6. James Cameron

7. Celine Dion

8. Cliff Thorburn

9. James Doohan

10. Born in Canada

TAKE A CHANCE 01

In this round each correct answer is worth 2 points making a possible score of 20. However if you get any question wrong your score for this round is halved. If you are not sure, leave an answer blank and you still score 2 points for each correct answer (unless you get one wrong!)

1. Nancy Wilkinson became the first winner of which famous TV quiz show in 1972?

2. Chester is situated on which river?

3. Who was the occasional partner of Les Dennis who tragically died in 1986?

4. Who wrote the novel "Tinker, Tailor, Soldier, Spy"?

5. Who was assassinated at the Ambassador Hotel in Los Angeles in June 1968?

6. Who won an Oscar for directing the film "Schindler's List"?

7. Starring Angela Lansbury, which TV series was set at Cabot Cove?

8. Which football club did Harry Enfield's kebab shop owner Stavros support?

9. Who was born in 1955 and at the age of 14 established the Lakeside Programming Club with some school friends?

10. Tom Hanks, Tim Allen and Don Rickles provided voices for which Disney film?

ANSWERS:

1. "Mastermind"

2. Dee

3. Dustin Gee

4. John Le Carre

5. Robert Kennedy

6. Stephen Spielberg

7. "Murder She Wrote"

8. Arsenal

9. Bill Gates

10. "Toy Story"

POT LUCK 02

1. Which famous London landmark is named after Benjamin Hall?

2. In which country is the Great Slave Lake?

3. Frances Gumm was the real name of which actress?

4. Mozzarella cheese is produced in which country?

5. In which Scottish city is Kelvingrove Art Gallery?

6. In which sport is the Stanley Cup contested?

7. Who wrote the play "Lady Windermere's Fan"?

8. Which football club did the League and Cup double for the second time in 1997 – 98?

9. What is the major export of Iceland?

10. In the fashion world what does DKNY stand for?

ANSWERS:

1. Big Ben

2. Canada

3. Judy Garland

4. Italy

5. Glasgow

6. Ice Hockey

7. Oscar Wilde

8. Arsenal

9. Fish (60% of export value)

10. Donna Karan New York

DISNEY FILMS

1. In which film does the Queen say, "Mirror, mirror on the wall, who is the fairest of them all"?

2. Phil Collins' Oscar winning song "You'll be in my Heart" was featured in which film?

3. Which Disney film featured kittens called Toulouse, Marie and Berlioz?

4. Which Disney film first featured Cruella De Vil?

5. Which actress starred in the film "Mary Poppins"?

6. Vanessa Williams hit "Colours of the Wind" was featured in which Disney film?

7. Mice called Gus and Jaq appeared in which Disney film?

8. What is the name of the bear in "The Jungle Book"?

9. Who provided the voice for Zazu the Hornbill in "The Lion King"?

10. What is the name of the boy who owns the toys in "Toy Story"?

ANSWERS:

1. "Snow White and the Seven Dwarfs"

2. "Tarzan"

3. "The Aristocats"

4. "101 Dalmatians"

5. Julie Andrews

6. "Pocahontas"

7. "Cinderella"

8. Baloo

9. Rowan Atkinson

10. Andy

CAPITAL CITIES

1. In which city are the headquarters of the international secretariat of NATO?

2. In which city did Oscar Wilde die?

3. In which European city is the Bernebau Stadium?

4. Haneda Airport serves which Asian city?

5. What is the largest city in Africa?

6. The South American football club Boca Juniors play their home games in which city?

7. Which was the first city to operate an underground rail network?

8. In which city was US President James Garfield assassinated?

9. Which European city stands on the River Vltava and features the 14th Century Charles Bridge?

10. If you flew to Kastrup Airport, which Scandinavian city would you be visiting?

ANSWERS:

1. Brussels

2. Paris

3. Madrid

4. Tokyo

5. Cairo

6. Buenos Aires

7. London

8. Washington DC

9. Prague

10. Copenhagen

FAMOUS PEOPLE

1. Which actor starred in the film "The Horse Whisperer"?

2. Which US President had a sign on his desk saying, "The buck stops here"?

3. Which singer's first UK No. 1 was "The Most Beautiful Girl" in 1994?

4. Who was the first Scot to become flat racing's Champion Jockey?

5. Which footballer and former England manager was nicknamed "Mighty Mouse"?

6. Which post-war Prime Minister won four General Elections?

7. Which member of the Beatles formed Wings?

8. Which actor provided the voice for "Count Duckula"?

9. Which author, broadcaster and animal collector's first book was "The Overloaded Ark"?

10. Who died after falling from his yacht the "Lady Ghislaine"?

ANSWERS:

1. Robert Redford

2. Harry Truman

3. Prince

4. Willie Carson

5. Kevin Keegan

6. Harold Wilson

7. Paul McCartney

8. David Jason

9. Gerald Durrell

10. Robert Maxwell

TAKE A CHANCE 02

In this round each correct answer is worth 2 points making a possible score of 20. However if you get any question wrong your score for this round is halved. If you are not sure, leave an answer blank and you still score 2 points for each correct answer (unless you get one wrong!)

1. San Marino forms an enclave within which country?

2. What food did the Owl & the Pussycat take on their voyage?

3. Who was the first British female singer to have a solo No 1 album in the UK charts?

4. Who was nicknamed 'The King of Ragtime'?

5. Who in 1963 gave his "I have a dream" speech in front of almost ½ million people in Washington DC?

6. In which 1989 film did Rick Moranis play Dr Wayne Szalinski?

7. Which "Coronation Street" character married Vicky Arden?

8. In "Harry Potter and the Chamber of Secrets", who was Slytherin's new seeker?

9. Who managed the Republic of Ireland to the 1988 European Championships?

10. Who composed the music – Gilbert or Sullivan?

ANSWERS:

1. Italy

2. Honey

3. Kate Bush

4. Scott Joplin

5. Martin Luther King

6. "Honey I Shrunk the Kids"

7. Steve McDonald

8. Draco Malfoy

9. Jack Charlton

10. Sullivan

POT LUCK 03

1. Which two countries lie on the Iberian Peninsula?

2. According to the saying, what is nine tenths of the law?

3. Sarah Jessica Parker played Carrie in which American TV series?

4. James Lofthouse created which sweets originally for trawlermen?

5. In which county is Cheddar Gorge?

6. What nationality was fashion designer Christian Dior?

7. What does the letter C stand for in YMCA?

8. Which stretch of water was crossed by the world's first commercial hovercraft service?

9. Aloha Airlines operate from which US state?

10. What does a topiarist design and form into ornamental shapes?

ANSWERS:

1. Portugal & Spain

2. Possession

3. "Sex and the City"

4. Fisherman's Friends

5. Somerset

6. French

7. Christian

8. English Channel

9. Hawaii

10. Shrubs (or Hedges)

WINTER SPORTS

1. Who was the first Englishman to win an Olympic Figure Skating title?

2. Which sport combines the disciplines of shooting and skiing?

3. Which Italian city hosted the 2006 Winter Olympics?

4. With which sport would you associate Alberto Tomba?

5. In which sport is a puck used?

6. In which sport did Eddie "The Eagle" Edwards make his name?

7. In which city were both Jayne Torvill and Christopher Dean born?

8. Name the British skier who was disqualified from the 2002 Olympic Slalom final after testing positive for a banned substance.

9. In which sport would a competitor perform a salchow?

10. In which sport would you throw stones at a house?

ANSWERS:

1. John Curry

2. Biathlon

3. Turin

4. Skiing

5. Ice Hockey

6. Ski Jumping

7. Nottingham

8. Alain Baxter

9. Ice Skating

10. Curling

TV 01

1. Which 1970's series starred James Bolam and Susan Jameson?

2. Who wrote and starred in the sitcom "dinnerladies"?

3. Which TV series starred Robert Vaughn and David McCallum?

4. In "Dad's Army" what was the first name of Sergeant Wilson?

5. Which TV series features the character Claude Jeremiah Greengrass?

6. Sam Malone was the central character in which TV series?

7. Who was sacked from "Have I Got News For You" in 2002?

8. What number is Dick Dastardly's 'Mean Machine' in the "Wacky Races"?

9. Which sitcom featured the characters Jim Trott and Owen Newitt?

10. What was the name of Lady Penelope's chauffeur?

ANSWERS:

1. "When The Boat Comes In"

2. Victoria Wood

3. "The Man from U.N.C.L.E."

4. Arthur

5. "Heartbeat"

6. "Cheers"

7. Angus Deayton

8. Double Zero

9. "The Vicar of Dibley"

10. Parker

G-MEN

1. Which actor played the title role in the 1992 film "Bram Stoker's Dracula"?

2. Which fashion designer was murdered in Miami in July 1997?

3. Which singer had No 1 hits in the 70's with "Clair" and "Get Down"?

4. Which former England manager once said, "Footballers are no different from human beings"?

5. Who in 1986 became the first American to win the Tour de France?

6. Which author wrote the "Flashman" series of books?

7. Leslie Lynch King Jr. was the original name of which US President?

8. Who was the original presenter of "The Krypton Factor"?

9. Which cricketer in 1990 created a record for the most runs scored in a single test match?

10. In 1942, who became leader of the US Army Air Force band in Europe?

ANSWERS:

1. Gary Oldman

2. Gianni Versace

3. Gilbert O'Sullivan

4. Graham Taylor

5. Greg Lemond

6. George Macdonald Fraser

7. Gerald Ford

8. Gordon Burns

9. Graham Gooch

10. Glenn Miller

TAKE A CHANCE 03

In this round each correct answer is worth 2 points making a possible score of 20. However if you get any question wrong your score for this round is halved. If you are not sure, leave an answer blank and you still score 2 points for each correct answer (unless you get one wrong!)

1. Which animal gives birth to the largest babies?

2. Which European country is home to the world's deepest cave?

3. Which song from Andrew Lloyd Webber's "Sunset Boulevard" became a 1993 hit for Dina Carroll?

4. Who became Chief Executive of the FA in 2003?

5. Name the Welsh Secretary who resigned after his "moment of madness" on Clapham Common in 1998.

6. Who is the only divorcee to become US President?

7. Which inventor was known as the Wizard of Menlo Park?

8. On which London station did WH Smith open his first stall selling books & newspapers in 1848?

9. Which annual sporting event did the BBC first broadcast live in 1938?

10. George Carey retired from which post in 2002 after 11 years in the job?

ANSWERS:

1. Blue Whale

2. France

3. "The Perfect Year"

4. Mark Palios

5. Ron Davies

6. Ronald Reagan

7. Thomas Edison

8. Euston

9. FA Cup Final

10. Archbishop of Canterbury

POT LUCK 04

1. What nationality was media tycoon Kerry Packer?

2. At which racecourse is the 1,000 Guineas run?

3. With which motor car company would you associate the Golf?

4. What is the chief export of South Africa by value?

5. In which county is the village of Cheddar?

6. Which athletics event takes place over a distance of 26 miles 385 yards?

7. Which newspaper broke the story of the alleged plot to kidnap Victoria Beckham in 2002?

8. Which animal is often referred to as 'the ship of the desert'?

9. James Bond shares a passionate moment with which long-serving character in "Die Another Day"?

10. Which racing driver was voted BBC Sports Personality of the Year in 1986 and 1992?

ANSWERS:

1. Australian

2. Newmarket

3. Volkswagen

4. Gold

5. Somerset

6. Marathon

7. News of the World

8. Camel

9. Miss Moneypenny

10. Nigel Mansell

GREAT SCOTS (Burns Night)

1. Which actor played Obi-Wan Kenobi in the film "Star Wars Episode 1: The Phantom Menace"?

2. Who managed Aberdeen to victory in the 1983 European Cup Winner's Cup final?

3. Who wrote the novel "Dr Jekyll & Mr Hyde"?

4. Which music hall singer was known for the song "Roamin' in the Gloamin'"?

5. Who was the founder of the Church of Scotland?

6. Which singer had her first single, "All This Time", go to No 1 in 2004?

7. Who is the only Scot to have been voted European Footballer of the Year?

8. Which Scot was Queen Victoria's servant and confidant from 1858?

9. Which Scot captained the British Lions on their tour of New Zealand in 1993?

10. Which comedian recorded the song "In The Brownies"?

ANSWERS:

1. Ewan McGregor

2. Alex Ferguson

3. Robert Louis Stevenson

4. Harry Lauder

5. John Knox

6. Michelle McManus

7. Denis Law

8. John Brown

9. Gavin Hastings

10. Billy Connolly

DOWN UNDER (Australia Day)

1. In which Australian city is the National Gallery?

2. Which Australian city is famous for its Opera House and Harbour Bridge?

3. Which beach takes its name from the Aboriginal word meaning "noise of water breaking over rocks"?

4. Which famous Australian bank robber was caught and hanged in 1880?

5. In which city is the Woolloongabba cricket ground?

6. Which Australian singer had a UK No. 1 with "Kiss Kiss" in 2002?

7. The city of Perth is situated on which river that also gives its name to a well known Aussie beer?

8. In which city does the Australian Open Tennis tournament take place?

9. The Great Barrier Reef is situated off the coast of which Australian state?

10. Which Australian city is named after King William IV's queen?

ANSWERS:

1. Canberra

2. Sydney

3. Bondi Beach

4. Ned Kelly

5. Brisbane

6. Holly Valance

7. Swan

8. Melbourne

9. Queensland

10. Adelaide

DOCS ON THE BOX

1. Hugh Laurie plays an antisocial maverick doctor in which US TV series?

2. Which actress played Dr Elizabeth Corday in "ER"?

3. Which character in "Cheers" married Dr Lilith Sternin?

4. Which 1980's TV series was set at Cooper's Crossing?

5. Which 1960's children's TV programme featured the character Dr Mopp?

6. Who played gynaecologist Dr Cliff Huxtable from 1984 – 92 in a US TV sitcom?

7. Which TV drama series is set at the Mill Surgery in the fictional Birmingham suburb of Letherbridge?

8. Who played Dr Mark Sloan in "Diagnosis Murder"?

9. The TV series "Trapper John MD" was a spin off from which American sitcom?

10. Which sci-fi series featured Robert Picardo as a holographic doctor?

ANSWERS:

1. "House"

2. Alex Kington

3. Frasier Crane

4. "The Flying Doctors"

5. "Camberwick Green"

6. Bill Cosby

7. "Doctors"

8. Dick Van Dyke

9. M*A*S*H

10. "Star Trek: Voyager"

TAKE A CHANCE 04

In this round each correct answer is worth 2 points making a possible score of 20. However if you get any question wrong your score for this round is halved. If you are not sure, leave an answer blank and you still score 2 points for each correct answer (unless you get one wrong!)

1. Which is the only football league club in England or Scotland whose name contains the letter J?

2. With which Indian city would you associate Mother Theresa?

3. In which film did Jane Horrocks impersonate Shirley Bassey, Barbra Streisand & Gracie Fields?

4. What is the name of Harry Potter's cousin with whom he lives?

5. In which decade was the halfpenny coin phased out?

6. Which 19-year-old British au pair had her conviction for murder overturned in a Massachusetts court in 1997?

7. The video to which song caused the Catholic Church to threaten Madonna with excommunication?

8. In which city is the Bellerive Oval, a recent addition to Australia's roster of Test venues?

9. Which artist entered an unmade bed for the 1999 Turner Prize?

10. Who frequently said, "Does my bum look big in this" on "The Fast Show"?

ANSWERS:

1. St Johnstone

2. Calcutta

3. "Little Voice"

4. Dudley Dursley

5. 1980's

6. Louise Woodward

7. "Like A Prayer"

8. Hobart

9. Tracy Emin

10. Arabella Weir

FEBRUARY

POT LUCK 05

1. Who scored the famous "Hand of God" goal at the 1986 World Cup?

2. On which continent are the Atlas Mountains?

3. ET are the international registration letters for cars from which country?

4. According to the proverb, what is the best policy?

5. Who wrote the comedy play "Jumpers" and co-wrote the screenplay for the film "Shakespeare in Love"?

6. What is the hobby of a toxophilite?

7. Tunisia has a coastline on which sea?

8. TV presenter Ulrika Jonsson was born in which Scandinavian country?

9. Which cartoon character is known as Miguel Ratonicito in Spain?

10. Which American Football team used to play their home games at Mile High Stadium?

ANSWERS:

1. Diego Maradonna

2. Africa

3. Egypt

4. Honesty

5. Tom Stoppard

6. Archery

7. Mediterranean

8. Sweden

9. Mickey Mouse

10. Denver Broncos (INVESCO Field at Mile High since 2001)

HISTORY

1. During which conflict did the Battle of St Albans take place?

2. Which cathedral saw the murder of Thomas À Becket in 1170?

3. The Warren Commission published a report on the assassination of which US President?

4. Catherine Howard and Jane Seymour were wives of which monarch?

5. Who was the last Tudor monarch of England?

6. Which US President survived an assassination attempt by John Hinckley?

7. During which war was the Atlantic Charter issued?

8. In which country did the Easter rising of 1916 take place?

9. Which US President was assassinated during a performance of the play "Our American Cousin"?

10. Which international prize was shared by Betty Williams and Mairead Corrigan in 1977?

ANSWERS:

1. Wars of the Roses

2. Canterbury

3. John F Kennedy

4. Henry VIII

5. Elizabeth I

6. Ronald Reagan

7. World War II

8. Ireland

9. Abraham Lincoln

10. Nobel Peace Prize

MORNING GLORY

1. Which group topped the album charts in 1995 with "(What's The Story) Morning Glory"?

2. Which Prime Minister had a yacht called "Morning Cloud"?

3. The song "Good Morning Starshine" featured in which controversial 60's musical?

4. Which group had a top 10 hit in 1977 with "Good Morning Judge"?

5. What was the newspaper the "Morning Star" previously known as?

6. Which Sheena Easton hit was released in the USA under the title "Morning Train"?

7. Who were the regular presenters of "This Morning" from 1988 to 2001?

8. Which singer had a top 10 hit in 1972 with "Morning Has Broken"?

9. Who was the star of the 1987 film "Good Morning Vietnam"?

10. How is the contraceptive drug Levonelle more popularly known?

ANSWERS:

1. Oasis

2. Edward Heath

3. "Hair"

4. 10cc

5. Daily Worker

6. "9 to 5"

7. Richard Madeley & Judy Finnigan

8. Cat Stevens

9. Robin Williams

10. Morning After Pill

SNOW CHANCE

1. The abominable snowman is said to inhabit which mountain range?

2. Which actress said, "I used to be Snow White, but I drifted"?

3. In which Southern Hemisphere country are the Snowy Mountains?

4. What was the title of the 1993 UK No.2 & US No. 1 for Canadian rapper Snow?

5. Which ITV series set in Skelthwaite featured Pam Ferris as Peggy Snow?

6. Who did John Snow play Test Match cricket for in the 60's & 70's?

7. Who wrote the children's story "The Snow Queen"?

8. Mark Snow had a UK No. 2 hit with the theme to which TV show?

9. On which channel has Jon Snow been the news anchorman since 1989?

10. Who wrote the fairy tale "Little Snow White"?

ANSWERS:

1. Himalayas

2. Mae West

3. Australia

4. "Informer"

5. "Where The Heart Is"

6. England

7. Hans Christian Andersen

8. "X-Files"

9. Channel 4

10. Brothers Grimm

TAKE A CHANCE 05

In this round each correct answer is worth 2 points making a possible score of 20. However if you get any question wrong your score for this round is halved. If you are not sure, leave an answer blank and you still score 2 points for each correct answer (unless you get one wrong!)

1. Dermatology is the study of what?

2. In which city is the Flat Iron Building, completed in 1902, at the junction of 5th Avenue & Broadway?

3. Who captained England to their first Test series victory for 31 years over the West Indies in 2000?

4. Who was the first reigning British monarch to visit China?

5. Which singer was known as "The Thin White Duke"?

6. Who is the Headmaster at Hogwarts School of Witchcraft & Wizardry?

7. Founded in 1694, what is sometimes known as "The Old Lady of Threadneedle Street"?

8. Which famous bear lives in the Hundred Acre Wood?

9. In "Thunderbirds", what colour was Lady Penelope's Rolls Royce?

10. In which film does Barbara Windsor's bra fly off when she is exercising?

ANSWERS:

1. Skin

2. New York

3. Nasser Hussein

4. Queen Elizabeth II

5. David Bowie

6. Albus Dumbledore

7. The Bank of England

8. Winnie the Pooh

9. Pink

10. "Carry on Camping"

POT LUCK 06

1. Ca is the chemical symbol for which element?

2. New Delhi is the capital of which country?

3. Which major US city was founded by William Penn in 1682?

4. In which city was the birthplace of St Paul?

5. Who was Vice-President of the USA from 1981 to 1989?

6. Which group had a No. 1 hit in 1996 with "How Deep Is Your Love"?

7. In which English city is the Castlefield Urban Heritage Park?

8. What type of animal is a Dandie Dinmont?

9. In Roman mythology, who performed twelve labours?

10. Which novel tells of Humbert Humbert's infatuation with a 12 year old girl?

ANSWERS:

1. Calcium

2. India

3. Philadelphia

4. Tarsus

5. George Bush

6. Take That

7. Manchester

8. Dog

9. Hercules

10. "Lolita"

ROMANCE (St Valentine's Day)

1. Which publishing company famous for romance novels was founded in 1908?

2. In which US series of the 1970s and 80s did passengers find romance aboard The Pacific Princess?

3. Which 1978 film musical features romances between the T-Birds and the Pink Ladies?

4. Which prolific author of romantic fiction, made a Dame in 1991, was known as the Queen of Romance?

5. Which actress, married to Michael Williams, co-starred with him in the TV comedy series "A Fine Romance"?

6. Which word can mean a vigorous Scottish dance or a short light-hearted romance?

7. The so-called Romance languages are descended from which ancient language?

8. Born in 1757, which English Romantic figure is famous as a poet, painter, and engraver?

9. Which 1997 film features the ill-fated romance of the characters Rose DeWitt Bukater and Jack Dawson?

10. Which British novelist and non-fiction writer wrote the romance 'Moll Flanders', published in 1722?

ANSWERS:

1. Mills & Boon

2. "Love Boat"

3. "Grease"

4. Barbara Cartland

5. Judi Dench

6. Fling

7. Latin

8. William Blake

9. "Titanic"

10. Daniel Defoe

SPORT ON FILM

1. Which city provides the setting for the 1996 film "When Saturday Comes"?

2. Which 1974 film starring Burt Reynolds features prisoners playing American Football?

3. Which basketball star appeared in the 1996 film "Space Jam"?

4. What was the result of the match in "Escape to Victory"?

5. Which 1993 film tells the story of the first ever Jamaican Olympic bobsled team?

6. Which actor played the part of Bob Champion in the 1983 film "Champions"

7. What sport is featured in the 1996 film "Tin Cup"?

8. Who played the coach of the Rockford Peaches in "A League of Their Own"?

9. Which sport features in the 1963 film "This Sporting Life"?

10. For which film did Robert De Niro gain 50 pounds for his portrayal of ageing boxer Jake La Motta?

ANSWERS:

1. Sheffield

2. "The Mean Machine" (or "The Longest Yard")

3. Michael Jordan

4. Draw (4 – 4)

5. "Cool Runnings"

6. John Hurt

7. Golf

8. Tom Hanks

9. Rugby League

10. "Raging Bull"

LOVE IS ALL AROUND (St Valentine's Day)

1. Which group topped the singles chart in 1994 with "Love is All Around"?

2. Which character in the TV series "Lovejoy" was played by Dudley Sutton?

3. Which band was fronted by Courtney Love from 1989 to 2002?

4. Who wrote the novel "Women in Love"?

5. Which singer had a top 3 hit in 1989 with "Love Changes Everything"?

6. Who recorded "Profoundly in Love with Pandora" for the "Adrian Mole" TV series?

7. Which actor played William Shakespeare in the 1999 film "Shakespeare in Love"?

8. What is the name of "Lady Chatterley's Lover"?

9. Which long running American series features Reverend Timothy Lovejoy amongst its multitude of characters?

10. Who spent 7 weeks at No 1 in the UK singles charts in 2007 with "Bleeding Love"?

ANSWERS:

1. Wet Wet Wet

2. 'Tinker' Dill

3. Hole

4. D H Lawrence

5. Michael Ball

6. Ian Dury

7. Joseph Fiennes

8. Oliver Mellors

9. "The Simpsons"

10. Leona Lewis

TAKE A CHANCE 06

In this round each correct answer is worth 2 points making a possible score of 20. However if you get any question wrong your score for this round is halved. If you are not sure, leave an answer blank and you still score 2 points for each correct answer (unless you get one wrong!)

1. What is the first name of Joan Collins' novelist sister?

2. Dollar had a Top 10 hit in 1979 with a cover version of which Beatles hit?

3. Majorca is the largest of which group of islands?

4. In which county is the Eden Project?

5. To date, John Travolta has had 2 Oscar nominations, name both films.

6. Who was the first member of England's World Cup winning team to be knighted?

7. Who was famous for her diet of curds and whey?

8. Which London nightclub was created in 1991 by Justin Berkmann and James Palumbo?

9. Which comedy partnership presented the surreal TV gameshow "Families at War"?

10. In "Fawlty Towers", why was Sybil in hospital when the party of Germans arrived?

ANSWERS:

1. Jackie

2. "I Wanna Hold Your Hand"

3. Balearic Islands

4. Cornwall

5. "Saturday Night Fever" & "Pulp Fiction"

6. Sir Bobby Charlton

7. Little Miss Muffett

8. Ministry of Sound

9. Vic Reeves & Bob Mortimer

10. Operation for an In-growing Toenail

POT LUCK 07

1. With which British city would you most associate the writers Alan Bleasdale, Phil Redmond and Carla Lane?

2. What is the name for a work of fiction which his longer than a short story but shorter than a novel?

3. What name is given to a baby whale?

4. Who provides the voice of Wallace in the "Wallace and Gromit" films?

5. Which valley in the Scottish highlands is also known as the "Great Glen"?

6. The SI unit of force is named after which scientist?

7. Castanets originate from which European country?

8. How many children does the Queen have?

9. In the song 'Widdecombe Fair', whose grey mare did the riders wish to borrow?

10. 'Never Tickle a Sleeping Dragon' is the motto of which fictional school?

ANSWERS:

1. Liverpool

2. Novella

3. Calf

4. Peter Sallis

5. Glen More (or Glen Albyn)

6. Sir Isaac Newton

7. Spain

8. 4

9. Tom Pearce

10. Hogwarts

MUSICALS

1. Julie Jordan is one of the central characters in which musical?

2. The song "I Remember It Well" was featured in which musical?

3. Which pop singer opened as Che Guevara in the musical "Evita" in 1978?

4. The musical "West Side Story" is set in which city?

5. Who wrote the script to the Queen musical "We Will Rock You"?

6. Which Andrew Lloyd Webber musical is based on the poems of TS Eliot?

7. Which musical is based on the story of "Madame Butterfly"?

8. Who wrote the musical "Annie Get Your Gun"?

9. The musical "Our House" featured the songs of which group?

10. The song "Secret Love" is featured in which musical?

ANSWERS:

1. "Carousel"

2. "Gigi"

3. David Essex

4. New York

5. Ben Elton

6. "Cats"

7. "Miss Saigon"

8. Irving Berlin

9. Madness

10. "Calamity Jane"

GENERAL KNOWLEDGE

1. What nationality is United Nations General Secretary Ban Ki-moon?

2. General Elections in the United Kingdom are traditionally held on which day?

3. In which sitcom did General Von Klinkerhoffen appear?

4. Where did General Custer make his last stand?

5. Who became General Secretary of the Soviet Communist party in 1922?

6. Who refused an Oscar for his portrayal of General George Patton in 1971?

7. Which TV quiz show features a round entitled 'General Ignorance'?

8. Which TV series featured a car called the General Lee?

9. In which year was the General Strike?

10. Who retired as a 4-star general in 1993 and was US Secretary of State from 2001 to January 2005?

ANSWERS:

1. South Korean

2. Thursday

3. 'Allo, 'Allo

4. Little Big Horn

5. Josef Stalin

6. George C Scott

7. "QI"

8. Dukes of Hazzard

9. 1926

10. Colin Powell

PLACES

1. In which US State is Cape Canaveral?

2. What is Finland's largest port?

3. Zulus mainly inhabit which country?

4. Carrasco Airport serves which Uruguayan city?

5. Which skyscraper in New York was completed in 1931 and was the world's tallest building for over 40 years?

6. In which country is Mount Cook National Park?

7. In which country are the Appalachian Mountains?

8. In which country was George Orwell born?

9. The soap opera "Hollyoaks" is set in which city?

10. In which Italian city is the Grand Canal?

ANSWERS:

1. Florida

2. Helsinki

3. South Africa

4. Montevideo

5. Empire State Building

6. New Zealand

7. United States of America

8. India

9. Chester

10. Venice

TAKE A CHANCE 07

In this round each correct answer is worth 2 points making a possible score of 20. However if you get any question wrong your score for this round is halved. If you are not sure, leave an answer blank and you still score 2 points for each correct answer (unless you get one wrong!)

1. According to the lyrics of which of his hits is Cliff Richard "going where the sea is blue"?

2. Which actor played detective Jack Frost on TV?

3. Who wrote "The Owl and the Pussycat"?

4. INTERNAL SCUM is an anagram of the name of which TV actor?

5. Where were Anne Boleyn and Catherine Howard executed?

6. Which city, approx 110 miles east of Los Angeles, was once known as 'The Playground of the Stars'?

7. Which controversial snooker player reportedly once said that he would have Dennis Taylor shot?

8. In which Carry On film did Fenella Fielding play the seductive vampire Valeria?

9. What is the duration of a period of play in a game of Ice Hockey?

10. Which High Street retailer began as a chain of 'penny bazaars' in Leeds with a loan of £5 from Isaac Dewhirst?

ANSWERS:

1. "Summer Holiday"

2. David Jason

3. Edward Lear

4. Martin Clunes

5. Tower of London

6. Palm Springs

7. Alex Higgins

8. "Carry On Screaming"

9. 20 minutes

10. Marks and Spencer

POT LUCK 08

1. The Mersey Tunnel links the town of Birkenhead with which city?

2. Which famous British Prime Minister died in 1965, aged 91?

3. A Kerry Blue is a breed of which animal?

4. How many innings does each side play in a game of baseball?

5. The town of Hay-on-Wye is famous as a centre for second-hand what?

6. From which English harbour did Francis Drake sail in 1588 to defeat the Spanish Armada?

7. Which two colours appear on the Spanish flag?

8. Which political party was founded in Munich, Germany in 1919?

9. In pre-decimal currency, how many farthings were there in a penny?

10. Emma Tennant's "Pemberley" is a sequel to which Jane Austen novel?

ANSWERS:

1. Liverpool

2. Sir Winston Churchill

3. Dog

4. 9

5. Books

6. Plymouth

7. Red & Yellow

8. Nazi Party (National Socialist Party)

9. 4

10. "Pride & Prejudice"

INITIAL SUCCESS 01

The first letter of each answer to questions 1 – 9 spells out the name of a place. Question 10 relates to that place.

1. In children's TV, what is the name of the cat that lives in the window of Emily's shop?

2. In which city did Sigmund Freud die in 1939?

3. What was the title of All Saints' 1997 debut album?

4. A string quartet features two violins, a viola and what?

5. Who keeps getting killed in the TV series "South Park"?

6. Captain Lindemann was in charge of which German ship when it sank in 1941?

7. Which chemical element with atomic number 92 is the heaviest naturally-occurring element?

8. Who was enthroned as the 104th Archbishop of Canterbury on February 27th 2003?

9. Which state traditionally holds the first primary elections in the US presidential campaign?

10. The Premier League football club from this town play at which ground?

ANSWERS:

1. Bagpuss

2. London

3. "All Saints"

4. Cello

5. Kenny

6. Bismarck

7. Uranium

8. Rowan Williams

9. New Hampshire

10. Ewood Park

TV TIMES

1. Which entertainer and comedian was the star of the 1994 comedy series "Time After Time"?

2. Who is the host on the Channel 4 series "Time Team"?

3. Which former "EastEnders" actor starred in the 2000 TV drama "Hero of the Hour"?

4. What was the main restriction on Michael Palin in his 1989 series "Around the World in 80 Days"?

5. What was the name of Judi Dench's character in the sitcom "As Time Goes By"?

6. Who plays Jack Bauer in the TV series "24"?

7. Who replaced Sir Robin Day as the chairman on "Question Time"?

8. Which actor played author Peter Mayle in the TV dramatisation of his book "A Year in Provence"?

9. What was the name of the character played by Ronnie Barker in "Open All Hours"?

10. On which TV series did you hear the words, "This tape will self destruct in five seconds"?

ANSWERS:

1. Brian Conley

2. Tony Robinson

3. Ross Kemp

4. No air travel

5. Jean

6. Keifer Sutherland

7. Peter Sissons

8. John Thaw

9. Arkwright

10. "Mission Impossible"

SCIENCE & NATURE

1. Which fluid lubricates the joints in the human body?

2. The gazelle naturally inhabits which continent?

3. What was the first antibiotic?

4. What is the term for pig's feet?

5. What is the more common name for Hansen's Disease?

6. What type of creature is a hammerhead?

7. Br is the chemical symbol for which element?

8. What is the term for the winter coat of a stoat?

9. In which part of the body do you have rods and cones?

10. What is the term for a person with an absence of the pigment melanin in the skin, hair and eyes?

ANSWERS:

1. Synovial Fluid

2. Africa

3. Penicillin

4. Trotters

5. Leprosy

6. Shark

7. Bromine

8. Ermine

9. Eyes

10. Albino

TAKE A CHANCE 08

In this round each correct answer is worth 2 points making a possible score of 20. However if you get any question wrong your score for this round is halved. If you are not sure, leave an answer blank and you still score 2 points for each correct answer (unless you get one wrong!)

1. Which fictional character has deceased parents called James and Lily?

2. Who developed an inoculation for smallpox?

3. Which Oasis song features the line "So I start a revolution from my bed"?

4. Which TV funny man created the Irish crooner Val Hooligan?

5. Who played the title role in the film "Annie Hall"?

6. What colour is the bottom band on the flag of India?

7. Which country has won the Rugby Union World Cup twice and not scored a try in either final?

8. Which building in Paris has blue air conditioning pipes, green water pipes and yellow fuse boxes and electricity cables?

9. Who was the only Chancellor of the Exchequer of the 20th Century never to deliver a budget speech to Parliament?

10. Which children's plaything took its name from the 26th President of the USA?

ANSWERS:

1. Harry Potter

2. Edward Jenner

3. "Don't Look Back in Anger"

4. Russ Abbot

5. Diane Keaton

6. Green

7. South Africa

8. Pompidou Centre

9. Iain MacLeod

10. Teddy Bear

MARCH

POT LUCK 09

1. What is the term applied to a large piece of music, literally meaning 'a sounding together'?

2. In Japan, the Yen is made up of one hundred what?

3. Which military dictator took control of Spain in 1936?

4. Vlad the Impaler was the historical inspiration for which gothic fictional character?

5. Dating from the Iron Age, what animal can be seen in chalk on a hillside at Uffington, in Oxfordshire?

6. What is the fictional land featured in the series of seven 'chronicles' for children by C S Lewis?

7. In Australia, what is the Aboriginal name for Ayers Rock?

8. A piano quintet is written for how many instruments?

9. Who won the Nobel Peace Prize in 1989 for his non-violent resistance to China?

10. Dunkery Beacon is the highest point of which national park in Devon and Somerset?

ANSWERS:

1. Symphony

2. Sen

3. General Franco

4. Count Dracula

5. Horse

6. Narnia

7. Uluru

8. 5

9. Dalai Lama

10. Exmoor

BRITAIN

1. Which current British national daily newspaper was first published in 1986?

2. Which London landmark appears on the front cover of the 1977 Pink Floyd album "Animals"?

3. The Brazilian footballer Juninho had three spells with which club in the north east of England?

4. Which British monarch succeeded George V?

5. What is the name of the UK government office where trademarks and copyrights are registered?

6. In Britain, how many copies must a single sell to earn a Silver Disc?

7. By what name is the sauce 'Crème Anglais' more commonly known in Britain?

8. What is a name for a sofa, an overcoat with a velvet collar and a town in Derbyshire?

9. Who served as British prime minister in between the two terms served by Harold Wilson?

10. In which British national park is Bala Lake?

ANSWERS:

1. The Independent

2. Battersea Power Station

3. Middlesbrough

4. Edward VIII

5. Patent Office

6. 200,000

7. Custard

8. Chesterfield

9. Edward Heath

10. Snowdonia

MOTHER'S DAY

1. According to the proverb, what is "the mother of invention"?
2. Which Spanish artist painted "Mother & Child" in 1921?
3. Which spirit is known as 'Mother's Ruin'?
4. Which 2005 film featured Jodie Foster as a mother whose daughter disappears on an aeroplane?
5. Actress Tippi Hedren is the mother of which actress?
6. Which group had a Top 5 hit in 1979 with "Does Your Mother Know"?
7. Who said in 1991, "the mother of all battles has begun"?
8. In Greek mythology, who unwittingly killed his father and married his mother?
9. Which Irish group founded Mother Records?
10. In pantomime, who is Aladdin's mother?

ANSWERS:

1. Necessity
2. Pablo Picasso
3. Gin
4. "Flightplan"
5. Melanie Griffith
6. Abba
7. Saddam Hussein
8. Oedipus
9. U2
10. Widow Twankey

WELSH WIZARDS (St. David's Day)

1. Which Prime Minister was called "The Welsh Wizard"?

2. Who is the singer and lead guitarist with the band Manic Street Preachers?

3. Which footballer won his 4th FA Cup winners medal in 1997?

4. Who won his 4th consecutive World Professional Snooker title in 1976?

5. Which singer was voted the Best British Male at the 2000 Brit Awards?

6. Who in 1999 became the first player to pass 1000 points in International Rugby Union?

7. Who wrote the 1940 short story collection "Portrait of the Artist as a Young Dog"?

8. Which actress starred in the 1999 film "Entrapment"?

9. Known as 'The Pride of Wales', won BBC Sports Personality of the Year 2007?

10. Which politician appeared in the video for Tracey Ullman's 1984 hit "My Guy"?

ANSWERS:

1. David Lloyd George

2. James Dean Bradfield

3. Mark Hughes

4. Ray Reardon

5. Tom Jones

6. Neil Jenkins

7. Dylan Thomas

8. Catherine Zeta Jones

9. Joe Calzaghe

10. Neil Kinnock

TAKE A CHANCE 09

In this round each correct answer is worth 2 points making a possible score of 20. However if you get any question wrong your score for this round is halved. If you are not sure, leave an answer blank and you still score 2 points for each correct answer (unless you get one wrong!)

1. Which group had Top 10 hits in the 1980's with "I'll Fly for You" and "Only When You Leave"?

2. Which haulage company gives all of its lorries girls' names?

3. Which actor played Idi Amin in the film "The Last King of Scotland"?

4. Which golfer won the USPGA Championship in the 1960's, 1970's and 1980's?

5. Which American intelligence organisation has its headquarters in Langley, Virginia?

6. Set in the 1950's, which TV show had several members of the cast attending Jefferson High School in Milwaukee?

7. Mrs Fluffytail was the mother of which character who appeared in the public information films of the 1960's and 1970's?

8. In which city are the headquarters of the American Express financial services group?

9. Who married John Melvin See Jr on 18th June 1962, gave birth to their daughter Heather on 31st December 1962 and divorced him in June 1965 before marrying a music legend on 12th March 1969?

10. "The Sons of the Desert" is an appreciation group for which famous comedy duo?

ANSWERS:

1. Spandau Ballet
2. Eddie Stobart Ltd
3. Forest Whitaker
4. Jack Nicklaus
5. CIA
6. "Happy Days"
7. Tufty
8. New York
9. Linda McCartney
10. Laurel & Hardy

POT LUCK 10

1. Which party won the 1997 General Election?

2. In Russia, the rouble is made up of one hundred what?

3. In musical theatre, which 'walk' is a song and dance number from 'Me and My Gal'?

4. What is the name of the famous glove puppet that has violent quarrels with his wife in a small booth?

5. In which English county would you find Sheringham and West Beckham?

6. Are there any snakes native to New Zealand?

7. What type of vehicle does the American company Boeing make?

8. The Trans-Siberian Express train travels between Vladivostok and which other Russian city?

9. What is the name of the pointed metal device used to secure a floating vessel to the sea bed?

10. What day do the French celebrate on the 14th of July every year?

ANSWERS:

1. Labour

2. Kopeks

3. "Lambeth Walk"

4. Mr Punch

5. Norfolk

6. No

7. Aircraft

8. Moscow

9. Anchor

10. Bastille Day

RELIGION

1. Who denied Christ three times on the night of Jesus' arrest?

2. How many points are on the 'Star of David'?

3. In the Christian calendar, what is the earliest date on which Easter Day can fall?

4. What name is given to a journey to a sacred place inspired by religious devotion?

5. In which language was the Koran written down?

6. In which religion is amrit referred to as the nectar of everlasting Life?

7. What was the name of the wooden box in which the Ten Commandments were placed?

8. What is the state of supreme bliss in Buddhism and Hinduism?

9. In which month is Saint Swithin's Day?

10. Which monarch, in 1534, styled himself head of the Church of England?

ANSWERS:

1. Peter

2. 6

3. March 22nd

4. Pilgrimage

5. Arabic

6. Sikhism

7. Ark of the Covenant

8. Nirvana

9. July (15th)

10. Henry VIII

SPORT

1. Which sporting event was first held in Athens in 1896?

2. In snooker, how many points are awarded to your opponent for a foul on the red ball?

3. Which British Heavyweight boxer was knighted by the Queen in February 2000?

4. Which North London football club has a cockerel standing on a ball as its crest?

5. Which famous baseball player was nicknamed the 'Bambino'?

6. Which equestrian event involves a series of tests involving complicated moves and halts?

7. Which French motor Racing world champion was nicknamed 'The Professor'?

8. In which English city is Headingley cricket ground?

9. In tennis, what is the next point won after 'deuce' called?

10. Who replaced Graham Taylor as England coach in 1994?

ANSWERS:

1. Olympic Games (Modern Era)

2. Four

3. Henry Cooper

4. Tottenham Hotspur

5. Babe Ruth

6. Dressage

7. Alain Prost

8. Leeds

9. Advantage

10. Terry Venables

COUNTIES

1. Who were England's opponents at the first Test Match at Durham's Riverside Cricket Ground in 2003?

2. Ray Dorset was the singer with which 1970's group?

3. Who wrote the poem "A Shropshire Lad"?

4. Which Scottish football club play their home games at Somerset Park?

5. In which city is the University of Central Lancashire?

6. Which author rode Devon Loch in the 1956 Grand National?

7. Which racecourse stages the Lincolnshire Handicap?

8. David Essex was once on the books of which football club?

9. Which TV series starred Alistair McKenzie, Richard Briers & Susan Hampshire?

10. The song "Surrey With A Fringe On Top" is featured in which musical?

ANSWERS:

1. Zimbabwe

2. Mungo Jerry

3. A E Houseman

4. Ayr United

5. Preston

6. Dick Francis

7. Doncaster

8. West Ham United

9. "Monarch of the Glen"

10. "Oklahoma"

TAKE A CHANCE 10

In this round each correct answer is worth 2 points making a possible score of 20. However if you get any question wrong your score for this round is halved. If you are not sure, leave an answer blank and you still score 2 points for each correct answer (unless you get one wrong!)

1. Which airline undertook a campaign of 'dirty tricks' against Richard Branson's Virgin Airline?

2. NATIVE NODDY is an anagram of the name of which film actor?

3. Which Tottenham Hotspur player scored twice in the 1981 FA Cup Final replay after being substituted in the first game?

4. What is the title of the TV drama series set in Africa and starring Stephen Tompkinson and Amanda Holden?

5. Which of the Queens children was nicknamed 'Jaws' at school because of the braces he wore on his teeth?

6. The coinage of which British Overseas Territory features the Gentoo Penguin, a sheep and a fox on the tails side?

7. "Just a week or two ago my dear old Uncle Bill. He went and kicked the bucket and left me in his will" are the opening lines to which famous song?

8. Which Soviet politician was Time Magazine's Person of the year twice in the 1980's?

9. Which actor was nominated for Oscars in four consecutive years in the 1970's?

10. Which US State is situated directly to the north of California?

ANSWERS:

1. British Airways
2. Danny DeVito
3. Ricky Villa
4. "Wild at Heart"
5. Prince Edward
6. Falkland Islands
7. "Any Old Iron"
8. Mikhail Gorbachev
9. Al Pacino
10. Oregon

POT LUCK 11

1. In Shakespeare's tragedy, 'Hamlet' is the prince of which country?

2. The singer Madonna had what surname at birth?

3. What was Emma's surname in the novel by Jane Austen?

4. What is added to Bacardi to make a Cuba Libre?

5. Bedfordshire Champion and Express Yellow are leading varieties of which vegetable?

6. According to Noel Coward's song, who along with "Englishmen go out in the midday sun"?

7. Which roast meat has a crisp, brown rind known as crackling?

8. Amadeus was the middle name of which composer?

9. Which BBC radio station was the first to broadcast nationally 24 hours a day?

10. What is the name of the dark pigment found in skin and hair?

ANSWERS:

1. Denmark

2. Ciccone

3. Woodhouse

4. Coca Cola

5. Onion

6. Mad Dogs

7. Pork

8. Mozart

9. Radio 2

10. Melanin

CARS (Start of the Grand Prix Season)

1. Which singer had a UK No. 1 with "Cars" in 1979?

2. Which car was advertised with the Groove Armada song "I See You Baby"?

3. The Volkswagen car company was founded in which country?

4. N is the international registration letter for cars from which country?

5. Which car company manufactures the Ibiza, Cordoba and Toledo?

6. What was the name of the Volkswagen in "The Love Bug"?

7. Which politician was nicknamed "Two Jags"?

8. Which motor car company is named after the founder of Detroit?

9. The car chase in the film "Bullitt" took place in which city?

10. According to the old advert, what make is "the car in front"?

ANSWERS:

1. Gary Numan

2. Renault Megane

3. Germany

4. Norway

5. Seat

6. Herbie

7. John Prescott

8. Cadillac

9. San Francisco

10. Toyota

DRAMA QUEENS

1. Which actress plays Susan Mayer in "Desperate Housewives"?

2. Which actress won 2 Golden Globes in 2007; one for playing Elizabeth I and the other for playing Elizabeth II?

3. Barbara-Ann Deeks was the real name of which actress?

4. Which actress played Alexis in "Dynasty"?

5. Who was the wife of "Dad's Army" actor John Le Mesurier?

6. Which actress played Purdey in "The New Avengers"?

7. Which actress played the title role in the TV series "Ally McBeal"?

8. Which "EastEnders" actress once said, "I'm too old for surgery. Is it worth it, to look good in your coffin"?

9. Who was John Cleese's wife who co-wrote "Fawlty Towers"?

10. Which actress plays Janice Battersby in "Coronation Street"?

ANSWERS:

1. Teri Hatcher

2. Helen Mirren

3. Barbara Windsor

4. Joan Collins

5. Hattie Jacques

6. Joanna Lumley

7. Calista Flockhart

8. June Brown

9. Connie Booth

10. Vicky Entwhistle

LOOK AT THE IRISH (St Patrick's Day)

1. In which sport did Irishman Willie John McBride achieve fame?

2. Which Irishman has hosted the Annual 'children In Need' appeal since 1980?

3. Which American actor appeared as the Irish gypsy One Punch Mickey in the 2000 Guy Ritchie film 'Snatch'?

4. Connemara is the western part of which Irish county?

5. Which Irish folksong provided a hit for the Pogues and the Dubliners in April 1987?

6. Which Irish nationalist political movement was founded by Arthur Griffiths early in the 20th Century?

7. Which Irish singer had a solo UK No 1 hit in 2002 with the single "Tomorrow Never Comes"?

8. Which Irish word is used for illegally distilled whiskey?

9. Which Irish city is the home of the Ulster Museum?

10. Which Irish writer created the characters Stephen Dedalus and Molly Bloom?

ANSWERS:

1. Rugby Union

2. Terry Wogan

3. Brad Pitt

4. County Galway

5. "The Irish Rover"

6. Sinn Fein

7. Ronan Keating

8. Poteen

9. Belfast

10. James Joyce

TAKE A CHANCE 11

In this round each correct answer is worth 2 points making a possible score of 20. However if you get any question wrong your score for this round is halved. If you are not sure, leave an answer blank and you still score 2 points for each correct answer (unless you get one wrong!)

1. Which actor played salesman Chris Gardner in the film "The Pursuit of Happyness"?

2. Which is the oldest of the British armed services?

3. Which illusionist famously made the Statue of Liberty disappear, levitated over the Grand Canyon and walked through the Great Wall of China?

4. Which famous film actress was nicknamed 'Hanoi Jane' after visiting North Vietnam in 1972?

5. "Naughty boys in nasty schools, headmasters breaking all the rules" is the opening line of which Madness hit?

6. The tune "Stone Fox Chase", by the Nashville band Area Code 615, was the distinctive theme to which rock music TV show?

7. In Scottish law there are 3 possible verdicts; guilty, not guilty and which other?

8. Who, in the 1960's, launched the "Clean Up TV" campaign?

9. Which legendary England boss took over as manager of Melchester Rovers while Roy Race was in a coma?

10. Which three digit number would you dial to hear the speaking clock?

ANSWERS:

1. Will Smith
2. Royal Navy
3. David Copperfield
4. Jane Fonda
5. "Baggy Trousers"
6. "Old Grey Whistle Test"
7. Not Proven
8. Mary Whitehouse
9. Sir Alf Ramsay
10. 123

POT LUCK 12

1. For what do the initials M.O.T stand when referring to the test of a car's roadworthiness?

2. What is an object that floats on water and is used to mark channels for shipping or warn of hazards?

3. West Point is a Military Academy in which country?

4. Which pop star married Debbie Rowe in Sydney in November 1996?

5. On which Caribbean island was Gloria Estefan born?

6. Which pre-decimalisation coin was known as a 'tanner'?

7. Which 1975 blockbuster film was based on a novel by Peter Benchley?

8. From which fish are rollmops made?

9. If a carnivorous animal eats meat, what is eaten by a nucivorous animal?

10. Which E.M. Forster novel involves a young Muslim doctor called 'Aziz'?

ANSWERS:

1. Ministry of Transport

2. Buoy

3. USA

4. Michael Jackson

5. Cuba

6. Sixpence

7. "Jaws"

8. Herring

9. Nuts

10. "A Passage to India"

THE FOUR SEASONS

1. Which actress won her 3rd Oscar for her performance in the 1968 film "The Lion in Winter"?

2. Which singer had a No 1 hit in 1963 with "Summer Holiday"?

3. Which British composer wrote "Spring Symphony"?

4. Which English poet wrote "To Autumn"? (Begins, "Season of mists and mellow fruitfulness")

5. Max de Winter is a central character in which novel?

6. Which soap opera is set in Summer Bay?

7. In which month does the Spring Bank Holiday fall?

8. "Forever Autumn" sung by Justin Hayward featured on which late 70's concept album?

9. The Winter Palace is situated in which Russian city?

10. The song "Summertime" is featured in which musical?

ANSWERS:

1. Katherine Hepburn

2. Cliff Richard

3. Benjamin Britten

4. John Keats

5. "Rebecca"

6. "Home & Away"

7. May

8. "Jeff Wayne's 'War of the Worlds'"

9. St Petersburg

10. "Porgy & Bess"

BOATS (University Boat Race)

1. What was the name of Malcolm Campbell's boat?

2. What was the name of Charles Darwin's ship?

3. What is the term for a small oval boat made by stretching hides over a wickerwork frame?

4. Captain Bligh was the victim of a mutiny on which ship?

5. Where does the University Boat Race finish?

6. Which ship in dry dock at Greenwich has a biennial tall ships race named after it?

7. Who wrote the novel "Three Men in a Boat"?

8. In which ship did the Pilgrim Fathers set sail in 1620?

9. What was the name of the boat Ellen MacArthur first sailed around the world solo?

10. What is the name of the flag flown on a ship about to set sail?

ANSWERS:

1. Bluebird

2. HMS Beagle

3. Coracle

4. Bounty

5. Mortlake

6. Cutty Sark

7. Jerome K Jerome

8. Mayflower

9. Kingfisher

10. Blue Peter

NICKNAMES

1. Which monarch was known as 'Bloody Mary'?

2. Which motor racing circuit in the USA is known as 'The Brickyard'?

3. Which composer was nicknamed 'The Red Priest'?

4. Which national daily newspaper is called 'The Thunderer'?

5. Which town is nicknamed 'Pompey'?

6. Which pop singer is nicknamed 'Alf'?

7. The 'Pumas' is the nickname of the rugby union team from which country?

8. What is the nickname of former Spice Girl Mel B?

9. Which football club is nicknamed 'The Rams'?

10. Which West Coast state is nicknamed 'The Golden State'?

ANSWERS:

1. Queen Mary I (NOT Mary, Queen of Scots)

2. Indianapolis

3. Antonio Vivaldi

4. The Times

5. Portsmouth

6. Alison Moyet

7. Argentina

8. Scary Spice

9. Derby County

10. California

TAKE A CHANCE 12

In this round each correct answer is worth 2 points making a possible score of 20. However if you get any question wrong your score for this round is halved. If you are not sure, leave an answer blank and you still score 2 points for each correct answer (unless you get one wrong!)

1. Who is the Patron Saint of Lovers?

2. Who was the leader of the suffragettes and founder of the Women's Social & Political Union?

3. Tom Chaplin is the lead singer with which English group?

4. What is the surname of the uncle and nephew who have won the World Cup for England at football and rugby union?

5. Which 1990's sitcom featured flat mates called Gary and Tony?

6. Which comedian starred in a TV series based on the works of Tony Hancock in the 90's?

7. Who was the first left-hander to win the World Professional Snooker Championship?

8. What is the name of the bell at Lloyd's rung to denote shipping losses?

9. What is the name of the cowgirl in the film "Toy Story 2"?

10. On which side of the road do the Japanese drive – right or left?

ANSWERS:

1. St Valentine

2. Emmeline Pankhurst

3. Keane

4. Cohen

5. "Men Behaving Badly"

6. Paul Merton

7. Mark Williams

8. Lutine Bell

9. Jessie

10. Left

APRIL

POT LUCK 13

1. In which English city is the Royal College of Music?

2. Who wrote "The Naked Civil Servant"?

3. Which word can precede box, release and cutting?

4. In 1990, John Major defeated Douglas Hurd and who else to become leader of the Conservative party?

5. In which US State is the city of Atlanta?

6. Bright's disease affects which part of the body?

7. Which country won the 1999 Rugby Union World Cup?

8. In Greek mythology, who was the father of Icarus?

9. Which American state is nicknamed the 'Empire State'?

10. Which group had a Top 10 hit in the 70's with "It's Only Rock and Roll"?

ANSWERS:

1. London

2. Quentin Crisp

3. Press

4. Michael Hestletine

5. Georgia

6. Kidneys

7. Australia

8. Daedalus

9. New York

10. Rolling Stones

CATS & DOGS

1. The Cheshire Cat featured in which film?

2. What was the name of the dog in "Oliver Twist"?

3. Which cartoon cat chased Tweety Pie?

4. What was the name of the first dog in space?

5. Which actress provided the voice for Zaza the cat in "Hector's House"?

6. In the "Back to the Future" films, Doc Emmett Brown's dog was named after which scientist?

7. Which Disney film feature cats called Si and Am?

8. Dogs called Perdita and Pongo featured in which Disney film?

9. With which cat would you associate cartoonist Jim Davis?

10. What was the name of the three-headed dog that guarded the Philosopher's Stone at Hogwarts School of Witchcraft & Wizardry?

ANSWERS:

1. "Alice in Wonderland"

2. Bullseye

3. Sylvester

4. Leika

5. Joanna Lumley

6. Einstein

7. "Lady and the Tramp"

8. "101 Dalmatians"

9. Garfield

10. Fluffy

HORSES (The Grand National)

1. In which sport is a pommel horse used?

2. In which city is the Spanish Riding School famous for its white Lippizaner horses?

3. Which member of the royal family fractured his shoulder in January 2001 after falling off his horse during a fox hunt?

4. According to the proverb, "If you can't ride two horses at once, you shouldn't be in the..." what?

5. Which comedian was the owner of the 1994 Grand National-winning horse, Miinnehoma?

6. Which boy's name comes from the Greek for 'lover of horses'?

7. 'Crazy Horse' was a leader of which Native American tribe?

8. Which jockey won the Epsom Derby on horses called Sir Ivor, Nijinsky and The Minstrel?

9. On which part of a horse is the fetlock?

10. Which horsemen, named from the Turkish for 'adventurer', lived in the south-west of the Russian Empire?

ANSWERS:

1. Gymnastics

2. Vienna

3. Prince Charles

4. Circus

5. Freddie Starr

6. Philip

7. Sioux

8. Lester Piggott

9. Leg

10. Cossacks

FOOLS (April Fool's Day)

1. If you were born on April Fool's Day, what would be your sign of the zodiac?

2. Which song was a Top 5 hit for both Frankie Lymon & the Teenagers and Diana Ross?

3. Which group topped the charts in 2000 with the single "Fool Again"?

4. Which British composer wrote the opera "The Perfect Fool" in 1921?

5. Which group had a Top 10 hit with "Fool To Cry" in 1976?

6. According to the proverb, a fool and his what are soon parted?

7. Which Oasis hit features the line, "Fool on the hill and I feel fine"?

8. In "Only Fools & Horses", which actor played Del Boy and Rodney's Uncle Albert?

9. Who had 80's hits with "Fool If You Think It's Over" and "No More The Fool"?

10. Complete this saying, "Fools rush in...

ANSWERS:

1. Aries

2. "Why Do Fools Fall In Love"

3. Westlife

4. Gustav Holst

5. Rolling Stones

6. Money

7. "D'You Know What I Mean"

8. Buster Merryfield

9. Elkie Brooks

10. Where Angels Fear to Tread

TAKE A CHANCE 13

In this round each correct answer is worth 2 points making a possible score of 20. However if you get any question wrong your score for this round is halved. If you are not sure, leave an answer blank and you still score 2 points for each correct answer (unless you get one wrong!)

1. Which US city suffered major earthquakes in 1906 and 1989?

2. Whitney Houston's hit "I Will Always Love You" was featured in which film?

3. Who was the first of the Beatles to have a solo UK No 1 single?

4. Who founded the Scout movement?

5. Which partnership wrote the song "A Policeman's Lot is not a Happy One"?

6. Who was the first snooker player to win the World Championship twice at the Crucible Theatre?

7. Which fictional detective is famous for using his "little grey cells"?

8. Characters called Sandra Hutchinson and Beryl Hennessey featured in which sitcom?

9. "To Bombay a travelling circus came" is the opening line of which children's song?

10. Where would you normally have seen Carol Hersey on TV?

ANSWERS:

1. San Francisco

2. "The Bodyguard"

3. George Harrison

4. Robert Baden Powell

5. Gilbert & Sullivan

6. Steve Davis (1981 & 1983)

7. Hercule Poirot

8. "The Liver Birds"

9. "Nellie the Elephant"

10. On The Test Card

POT LUCK 14

1. In which country was Omar Sharif born?

2. Which monarch led the English at Agincourt in 1415?

3. Who wrote the novel "Animal Farm"?

4. Which percussion instrument has varieties called bass, kettle and snare?

5. Which football club plays their home games at Ashton Gate?

6. What nationality was designer Pierre Cardin?

7. With which sport would you associate Adrian Moorhouse?

8. Which country is the world's leading producer of rice?

9. What is the official language of Iraq?

10. What is the art of producing miniature trees by selective pruning?

ANSWERS:

1. Egypt

2. Henry V

3. George Orwell

4. Drums

5. Bristol City

6. French

7. Swimming

8. China

9. Arabic

10. Bonsai

HEROES & VILLAINS

1. Which actor played Elliot Ness in the film "The Untouchables"?
2. Who was Sherlock Holmes' arch enemy?
3. What was Johnny Weismuller's most famous film role?
4. Which actor played Lex Luthor in the "Superman" films?
5. What was the other identity of Peter Parker?
6. Who was nicknamed "Public Enemy Number One" by the FBI in the 1930's?
7. Who is the sea captain in the series of novels by Patrick O'Brian that started with "Master & Commander" in 1970?
8. Who led the Gunpowder Plot?
9. Who is the leader of the X-Men?
10. Who murdered his wife, variety artist Belle Elmore?

ANSWERS:

1. Kevin Costner
2. Professor Moriarty
3. Tarzan
4. Gene Hackman
5. Spiderman
6. John Dillinger
7. Jack Aubrey
8. Robert Catesby
9. Professor Charles Xavier
10. Dr Crippen

MUSIC

1. Who wrote the musical "Anything Goes"?

2. Which singer had a No 1 hit in 1981 with "Begin the Beguine"?

3. Abba won the 1974 Eurovision Song Contest with which song?

4. With which style of music would you associate Glyndebourne?

5. Which actor had a hit single with "I Could Be So Good For You", the theme from "Minder"?

6. With which style of music would you associate Randy Travis?

7. Which singer had a Top 3 hit in 1987 with "My Baby Just Cares For Me"?

8. The song "Food, Glorious Food" is featured in which musical?

9. What was the Australian national anthem before "Advance Australia Fair"?

10. What nationality was Mozart?

ANSWERS:

1. Cole Porter

2. Julio Iglesias

3. "Waterloo"

4. Opera

5. Dennis Waterman

6. Country

7. Nina Simone

8. "Oliver"

9. "God Save The Queen" (Changed in 1984)

10. Austrian

EASTER

1. What type of headwear is shown off in an Easter Parade at Battersea every year?

2. According to the Book of Acts, how many days after Easter did the Ascension take place?

3. Easter Road Stadium is the home ground of which Scottish Premier club?

4. To which South American country does Easter Island belong?

5. Who co-starred with Fred Astaire in the 1948 musical "Easter Parade"?

6. What name is given to the Thursday before Easter Day?

7. In which sport is there an annual race from Devizes to Westminster at Easter?

8. In which country did the 1916 Easter Rising take place?

9. Which jeweller made famous gold and jewel-encrusted Easter eggs for the Russian royal family?

10. In Europe, the meat of which young animal is traditionally served at Easter?

ANSWERS:

1. Bonnets or Hats

2. 40

3. Hibernian

4. Chile

5. Judy Garland

6. Maundy Thursday

7. Canoeing

8. Ireland

9. Peter Carl Fabergé

10. Lamb

TAKE A CHANCE 14

In this round each correct answer is worth 2 points making a possible score of 20. However if you get any question wrong your score for this round is halved. If you are not sure, leave an answer blank and you still score 2 points for each correct answer (unless you get one wrong!)

1. How many people did Jesus feed with 5 loaves and 2 fishes?

2. Captain America and Billy are the central characters in which 1969 cult movie?

3. What was the real name of the "Elephant Man"?

4. Which two composers are Cockney rhyming slang for "drunk"?

5. Which 1980's pop group is perhaps best remembered for the flamboyant haircut of lead singer Mike Score?

6. Zulus mainly inhabit which country?

7. At the age of 39, which former champion reached the semi-finals of the US Open tennis tournament in 1991 after entering as a wild card?

8. In which country is the Bay of Plenty?

9. The musical "West Side Story" is based on which Shakespeare play?

10. Sideshow Bob is a criminal character in which TV show?

ANSWERS:

1. 5000

2. "Easy Rider"

3. John Merrick

4. Brahms & Liszt

5. A Flock of Seagulls

6. South Africa

7. Jimmy Connors

8. New Zealand

9. "Romeo & Juliet"

10. "The Simpsons"

POT LUCK 15

1. The food additive 'Monosodium Glutamate' is often abbreviated to what?

2. Nefertiti was queen of which country in the fourteenth century BC?

3. Which US city has the highest population?

4. Which illegal drug was first produced in Germany in 1898 as an analgesic?

5. The Roman Emperor Vespasian ordered the construction of which famous Amphitheatre in Rome?

6. Which keyboard instrument has pipes, bellows and stops?

7. Which Scottish author wrote 'Trainspotting' and 'Filth'?

8. In which industry is Bruce Oldfield a leading name?

9. In A A Milne's 'Winnie the Pooh' stories, what is the name of the little boy?

10. Which tree is named from the belief that one of the Apostles hanged himself from its branches?

ANSWERS:

1. MSG

2. Egypt

3. New York

4. Heroin

5. Coliseum

6. Organ

7. Irvine Welsh

8. Fashion Design

9. Christopher Robin

10. Judas Tree

WORLD CHAMPIONS

1. Leighton Rees was the first ever world champion in which sport?

2. Who won the World Snooker title at his first attempt in 1979?

3. Karen Briggs was 4 times World Champion in the under 48kg Class of which sport?

4. Which athlete won the Men's 100m at the first 3 World Championships?

5. At which weight was Barry McGuigan a world champion – lightweight, featherweight or bantamweight?

6. Jansher and Jahangir Khan have between them won 14 World Titles in which sport?

7. Which Brazilian driver won his first Formula 1 World Championship in 1988?

8. At which sport was Permin Zurbriggen a double world champion in 1987?

9. Which Briton won the World Superbike Championship in 2007?

10. Fred Couples won the first ever World Championship held for which sport?

ANSWERS:

1. Darts

2. Terry Griffiths

3. Judo

4. Carl Lewis

5. Featherweight

6. Squash

7. Ayrton Senna

8. Skiing (Slalom & Giant Slalom)

9. James Toseland

10. Golf

POP SINGERS

1. Who was the vocalist with the Police?

2. Which singer had hits in the 90's with "Change" and "Live Together"?

3. Which singer's 6th UK No 1 single was "Slow" in 2003?

4. Which member of Thin Lizzy died in January 1986?

5. Which singer had top 5 hits in 1969 with "For Once in My Life" and "My Cherie Amour"?

6. Which singer topped the charts in 1999 with "Baby One More Time"?

7. Which singer has recorded hit singles with Cliff Richard, John Travolta & the Electric Light Orchestra?

8. Which singer had No 1 albums in the 70's with "Atlantic Crossing" and "A Night on the Town"?

9. Which singer starred in the 2002 film "8 Mile"?

10. Which singer had No 1 hits in 1996 with "Flava" and "I Feel You"?

ANSWERS:

1. Sting

2. Lisa Stansfield

3. Kylie Minogue

4. Phil Lynott

5. Stevie Wonder

6. Britney Spears

7. Olivia Newton-John

8. Rod Stewart

9. Eminem

10. Peter Andre

EAST & WEST

1. In which country is the port of East London?

2. Which TV hero was played by Adam West?

3. Which town between Glasgow and Edinburgh is home to East Stirling Football Club?

4. In which US state is Key West?

5. The University of East Anglia opened in which city in 1962?

6. Which group had a Top 3 album in 1982 with "Pelican West"?

7. Who wrote the novel "East of Eden"?

8. Which West Indies cricketer set a world record for a single test innings against England in 2004?

9. Which Middle Eastern city is nicknamed 'The Pearl of the East'?

10. In which US state is West Point?

ANSWERS:

1. South Africa

2. Batman

3. Falkirk

4. Florida

5. Norwich

6. Haircut 100

7. John Steinbeck

8. Brian Lara

9. Damascus

10. New York

TAKE A CHANCE 15

In this round each correct answer is worth 2 points making a possible score of 20. However if you get any question wrong your score for this round is halved. If you are not sure, leave an answer blank and you still score 2 points for each correct answer (unless you get one wrong!)

1. In geometry, how many sides has an octagon?

2. Which Shakespeare play features the line, "Now is the winter of our discontent"?

3. On which island were the members of the Bee Gees born?

4. Which legendary comedy trio had the first names Larry, Curly and Moe?

5. Which British jockey won the Prix De L'Arc de Triomphe four times in the 1980's?

6. Which TV series featured a car called the General Lee?

7. When Neil Kinnock was appointed leader of the Labour Party, who became his deputy?

8. Bobby Farrell, Marcia Barrett, Liz Mitchell & Maisie Williams formed which chart topping 70's group?

9. Which actor played Britain's most famous executioner in the 2006 film "Pierrepoint"?

10. In Mia Farrow's autobiography, which famous singer did she claim offered to have Woody Allen's legs broken when he was found to be having an affair with her adopted daughter?

ANSWERS:

1. Eight
2. "Richard III"
3. Isle of Man
4. The Three Stooges
5. Pat Eddery
6. "Dukes of Hazzard"
7. Roy Hattersley
8. Boney M
9. Timothy Spall
10. Frank Sinatra

POT LUCK 16

1. Which part of the eye controls the amount of light entering the pupil?

2. Which Derby-winning racehorse was kidnapped in 1983?

3. Who is traditionally regarded as the patron saint of travellers?

4. Moss Side is a residential district in which Northern city?

5. In J.M. Barrie's "Peter Pan" what noisy object had the crocodile swallowed?

6. In nature, a ginkgo is a type of what?

7. Which castle, on the river Dee in Scotland, is a private residence of the Queen?

8. In which US sport do teams compete for the Super Bowl?

9. In the nursery rhyme, who '...met a pie man going to the fair'?

10. The 'Altair Eight Thousand Eight Hundred' was the first type of what electronic device?

ANSWERS:

1. Iris

2. Shergar

3. St Christopher

4. Manchester

5. Clock

6. Tree

7. Balmoral

8. American Football

9. Simple Simon

10. Personal Computer

BY GEORGE (St George's Day)

1. Who play home test matches at the Bourda Cricket Ground in Georgetown?

2. Who plated Queen Charlotte in the 1994 film "The Madness of King George"?

3. Complete this well-known saying, Lloyd George knew…"?

4. For which film did ageing comedian George Burns win a Best Supporting Actor Oscar in 1976?

5. Which king instituted the George Cross medal? (NAME & NUMBER)

6. Which character was played by George Wendt in "Cheers"?

7. From which Shakespeare play is the following quote taken, "Cry God for Harry, England and St George"?

8. What was the title of the Batman film that starred George Clooney?

9. Charlie George scored the winning goal for which team in the 1971 FA Cup Final?

10. What does the W stand for in George W Bush?

ANSWERS:

1. West Indies

2. Helen Mirren

3. My Father

4. "The Sunshine Boys"

5. George VI (1940)

6. Norm Peterson

7. Henry V

8. "Batman & Robin"

9. Arsenal

10. Walker

ENTERTAINMENT

1. With which musical instrument would you associate Johnny Dankworth?

2. Who won the 1983 Pulitzer Prize for the novel "The Colour Purple"?

3. Which Radio 1 disc jockey refused to play "Relax" by Frankie Goes to Hollywood?

4. Which singer had a No 1 hit in 1983 with "Wherever I Lay My Hat (That's My Home)"?

5. Which actor starred alongside Dan Ackroyd in the film "Blues Brothers 2000"?

6. What nationality was composer Antonio Vivaldi?

7. The Naughty Pigs are a constant nuisance to which children's TV character?

8. On which radio show is a guest allowed to choose 8 records, a book and a luxury item?

9. Which rock group had a top 10 hit in 1992 with "Viva Las Vegas"?

10. Which actress starred in the film "One Million Years BC"?

ANSWERS:

1. Saxophone

2. Alice Walker

3. Mike Read

4. Paul Young

5. John Goodman

6. Italian

7. Shaun the Sheep

8. "Desert Island Discs"

9. ZZ Top

10. Racquel Welch

RIVERS

1. Who composed "The Blue Danube"?

2. The song "Old Man River" is about which river?

3. Which group had a hit with "Ferry Across the Mersey" in the 1960's?

4. Which footballer had a top 3 hit in 1990 with "Fog on the Tyne"?

5. Tower Bridge is situated on which river?

6. The Amazon flows into which ocean?

7. In which city is Trent Bridge cricket ground?

8. Who wrote the novel "Death on the Nile"?

9. Which singer had a No 1 hit in 1988 with "Orinoco Flow"?

10. Which actor won an Oscar for his performance in the film "Bridge on the River Kwai"?

ANSWERS:

1. Johann Strauss

2. Mississippi

3. Gerry and the Pacemakers

4. Gazza (Paul Gascoigne)

5. Thames

6. Atlantic

7. Nottingham

8. Agatha Christie

9. Enya

10. Alec Guinness

TAKE A CHANCE 16

In this round each correct answer is worth 2 points making a possible score of 20. However if you get any question wrong your score for this round is halved. If you are not sure, leave an answer blank and you still score 2 points for each correct answer (unless you get one wrong!)

1. In which decade were Access credit cards introduced in the UK?

2. Which actress played the title role in the 2005 film "Nanny McPhee"?

3. In the phonetic alphabet, which word represents the letter X?

4. In which song was Glen Campbell, "riding out on a horse in a star spangled rodeo"?

5. Which sporting milestone was created at an athletics meeting between the Amateur Athletic Association and the University Athletic Association in 1954?

6. Which famous hangman executed Lord Haw Haw, Ruth Ellis and Derek Bentley?

7. Funny man Charles Penrose is best associated with a famous recording of which song?

8. Which "Friends" star was treated for an addiction to painkillers in 1997?

9. What colour leotard was famously worn by fitness guru Diana Moran in the 1980's?

10. Which children's TV programme featured Great Uncle Bulgaria and Bungo?

ANSWERS:

1. 1970's
2. Emma Thompson
3. X-Ray
4. "Rhinestone Cowboy"
5. First sub 4 minute mile
6. Albert Pierrepoint
7. "The Laughing Policeman"
8. Matthew Perry
9. Green
10. "The Wombles"

MAY

POT LUCK 17

1. In which country does Parmesan cheese originate?

2. What type of clothing is a 'Fedora'?

3. Which metal is combined with lead to make solder?

4. Which country has a coastline on both the Atlantic and Indian Oceans?

5. Idris the Dragon was a character from which children's TV programme?

6. In medicine, 'anti-tussive' drugs relieve or prevent what?

7. Which imaginary line divides the Earth into the Northern and Southern hemispheres?

8. The Clifton Suspension Bridge spans which British river?

9. In gardening, which 'H' is a word used to describe a plant which can survive frosts?

10. A human being has seven vertebrae in the neck; how many does a giraffe have?

ANSWERS:

1. Italy

2. Hat

3. Tin

4. South Africa

5. "Ivor the Engine"

6. Coughing

7. Equator

8. Avon

9. Hardy

10. Seven

MAY DAY

1. Who played the role of 'Pop' Larkin in the TV series 'The Darling Buds of May'?

2. Which film, based on a Louisa May Alcott novel, starred Winona Ryder and Susan Sarandon as part of the March family?

3. Which car firm used to manufacture a model called the Mayflower in the early 1950's?

4. Former England cricket captain, Peter May, captained which county to seven consecutive county championships?

5. Which Lerner & Loewe musical features the songs "The Lusty Month of May" and "How to Handle a Woman"?

6. The 'Mayflower Steps' are a tourist attraction in which south-western English city?

7. Which TV series is presented by James May, Richard Hammond and Jeremy Clarkson?

8. Who had hit singles in the 1970's with "Maggie May" and "Sailing"?

9. To which political party does Theresa May belong?

10. Brian May, Roger Taylor and John Deacon were members of which rock group?

ANSWERS:

1. David Jason
2. "Little Women"
3. Triumph
4. Surrey
5. Camelot
6. Plymouth
7. "Top Gear"
8. Rod Stewart
9. Conservative
10. Queen

INITIAL SUCCESS 02

The first letter of each answer to questions 1 – 9 spells out a person's name. Question 10 relates to that person.

1. Which actor starred in the TV series "Crocodile Shoes"?

2. Which Englishman played against Nottingham Forest in the 1980 European Cup Final?

3. Which novel is based on the experiences of Alexander Selkirk?

4. On which London street is Selfridge's?

5. Which club was the first to win all 4 divisions of the Football League?

6. In the book "Treasure Island", the parrot belonging to which character often said, "Pieces of Eight"?

7. Which cricketer undertook a charity walk from John O'Groats to Land's End for leukaemia research in 1985?

8. Who was the original presenter of "Sale of the Century"?

9. Which former actress is the MP for Hampstead and Highgate?

10. What is her first name?

ANSWERS:

1. Jimmy Nail

2. Kevin Keegan

3. "Robinson Crusoe"

4. Oxford Street

5. Wolverhampton Wanderers

6. Long John Silver

7. Ian Botham

8. Nicholas Parsons

9. Glenda Jackson

10. Joanne

FICTIONAL DETECTIVES

1. What was Inspector Clouseau's first name?

2. Agatha Christie's first detective novel was "The Mysterious Affair at Style's". Who did it feature?

3. Gill Grissom leads the Crime Scene Investigation team in which US city?

4. Which detective first appeared in the 1887 novel "A Study in Scarlet"?

5. Who created Mike Hammer?

6. Which police inspector patrols the streets of the English town of Denton?

7. What was the name of Eddie Murphy's character in the "Beverley Hills Cop" films?

8. Which 12th Century Welsh monk lives at Shrewsbury Abbey and uses his great powers of deduction to solve murder mysteries?

9. Name the private eye played by Humphrey Bogart in the 1941 film "The Maltese Falcon"?

10. What type of gun did San Francisco cop Harry Callahan carry?

ANSWERS:

1. Jacques

2. Hercule Poirot

3. Las Vegas

4. Sherlock Holmes

5. Mickey Spillane

6. Inspector Frost

7. Axel Foley

8. Brother Cadfael

9. Sam Spade

10. .44 Magnum

TAKE A CHANCE 17

In this round each correct answer is worth 2 points making a possible score of 20. However if you get any question wrong your score for this round is halved. If you are not sure, leave an answer blank and you still score 2 points for each correct answer (unless you get one wrong!)

1. Walt Disney won one full sized Oscar & 7 miniature Oscars for which of his films?

2. Which comedian used the catchphrase "Hello playmates"?

3. Whose novels are set in Discworld?

4. Who wrote the "Just William" books?

5. Which actress said, "I've only slept with men I've been married to. How many women can make that claim"?

6. Which retired tennis player once said, "I feel old when I see mousse in my opponent's hair"?

7. Which TV series featured DI Susan Alembic and DS Luke Stone?

8. Miss Lemon is the secretary of which fictional sleuth?

9. True or False – Adolf Hitler's mother considered having an abortion but was talked out of it by her doctor?

10. Which religious leader was named an "Honorary Harlem Globetrotter" in 2000?

ANSWERS:

1. "Snow White & the Seven Dwarfs"

2. Arthur Askey

3. Terry Pratchett

4. Richmal Crompton

5. Elizabeth Taylor

6. Andre Agassi

7. "Murder City"

8. Hercule Poirot

9. True

10. Pope John Paul II

POT LUCK 18

1. In which village were the antics of 'Noel's House Party' said to take place?

2. The British Standards Institute uses what mark as a sign of approval?

3. Which tabloid newspaper was launched in 1964?

4. What was the real name of the Scottish nationalist nicknamed 'Braveheart'?

5. Which book by Richard Adams features the characters Hazel, Fiver and Bigwig?

6. Which pop band had a U.K. hit in 1995 with 'Country House'?

7. Found in the leg, the tendon that joins the heel and calf is named after which Greek hero?

8. What name was nuclear plant Windscale changed to in 1971?

9. In which sport are David Howell and Lee Westwood professionals?

10. The Beat Generation was a literary movement founded in which decade?

ANSWERS:

1. Crinkly Bottom

2. Kite Mark

3. The Sun

4. William Wallace

5. "Watership Down"

6. Blur

7. Achilles

8. Sellafield

9. Golf

10. 1950's

MUSIC ON TV

1. Which pop star hosted the Channel 5 show "Night Fever"?

2. Who was the female presenter of the 1970's pop music show "Lift Off"?

3. Which group formed the panel on "Juke Box Jury" on 7th December 1963?

4. Who was the first presenter of the pop quiz show "Never Mind the Buzzcocks"?

5. Who won the second series of "Pop Idol" in 2003?

6. Which Dire Straits video was the first shown on MTV Europe?

7. Which rock music show was presented by Jools Holland and Paula Yates?

8. In 1972, Bob Harris became the presenter of which rock music programme?

9. Which TV show featured the dance troupe Legs and Co?

10. Who was the host of the TV show "My Kind of Music" from 1997 to 2002?

ANSWERS:

1. Suggs

2. Ayesha Brough

3. Beatles

4. Mark Lamarr

5. Michelle McManus

6. "Money for Nothing"

7. "The Tube"

8. "Old Grey Whistle Test"

9. "Top of the Pops"

10. Michael Barrymore

THE A LIST

1. Who led the Greeks at the siege of Troy?

2. What is the name of the cartoon hero created by Frenchmen Rene Goscinny & Albert Uderzo?

3. What is called Uluru by Australian aborigines?

4. What was the name of the Muslim sect that murdered Christians in the 11th – 14th centuries?

5. Which Scottish football club play their home games at Pittodrie?

6. Which computer and electronics company was founded by Alan Sugar?

7. Which hero of "The Arabian Nights" uses the words "open sesame"?

8. Zaragoza is the capital of which region of Spain?

9. What is the name of the American national burial ground and national shrine in Virginia?

10. Which British band was formed in 1977 by Stuart Leslie Goddard?

ANSWERS:

1. Agamemnon

2. Asterix the Gaul

3. Ayers Rock

4. Assassins

5. Aberdeen

6. Amstrad

7. Ali Baba

8. Aragon

9. Arlington National Cemetery

10. Adam & the Ants

ANIMAL WORLD

1. Which animal, often kept as a pet, is known as the Sand Rat or Desert Kangaroo?

2. Which is the only mammal to be able to kneel on all fours?

3. What is the name given to monkeys with blue and red bottoms?

4. What are rhino's horns made from?

5. How much water can a pelican hold in its beak – 3, 5 or 7 gallons?

6. Whales live in groups of up to 50, what are the groups called?

7. Which is the largest of the American big cats?

8. Who has the most chromosomes – Tarzan, Jane or Cheetah?

9. Which animal can be 'Blue Imperial', 'New Zealand' or 'Angora'?

10. TRUE or FALSE – the first dog to be fitted with contact lenses was run over the next day.

ANSWERS:

1. Gerbil

2. Elephant

3. Mandrills

4. Hair

5. 3 Gallons

6. Pods

7. Jaguar

8. Cheetah

9. Rabbits

10. True

TAKE A CHANCE 18

In this round each correct answer is worth 2 points making a possible score of 20. However if you get any question wrong your score for this round is halved. If you are not sure, leave an answer blank and you still score 2 points for each correct answer (unless you get one wrong!)

1. Which actor was the father of actress Jane Fonda?

2. What is the Russian term for an astronaut?

3. Which actor starred in the 1989 film "Dead Poet's Society"?

4. With which ventriloquist would you associate Lord Charles?

5. What is the highest mountain in the Grampians?

6. Clare Grogan was the singer with which 1980's pop group?

7. Which German tennis player won her first Wimbledon Ladies Singles title in 1988?

8. Which politician was famously grilled by Gloucestershire housewife Diana Gould on the TV show "Nationwide" over the sinking of the General Belgrano?

9. What are the only mammals that can fly?

10. Who succeeded Helmut Kohl as Chancellor of Germany in 1998?

ANSWERS:

1. Henry Fonda

2. Cosmonaut

3. Robin Williams

4. Ray Allen

5. Ben Nevis

6. Altered Images

7. Steffi Graf

8. Margaret Thatcher

9. Bats

10. Gerhard Schroeder

POT LUCK 19

1. Topside is a joint of which meat?

2. Cox's Cave and Jacob's Ladder are amongst the features of which Somerset tourist attraction?

3. In Greek mythology, which mountain is traditionally regarded as the home of the Greek gods?

4. The 2003 film 'Calendar Girls' was about a nude calendar featuring members of which organisation?

5. Which country's World War I troops were nicknamed 'Doughboys'?

6. In netball, how many players on a team are allowed to score?

7. Who assumed the presidency of Chile in 1973 after a military coup?

8. What was the first name of Sherlock Holmes's friend Dr Watson?

9. In Roman times, what was a denarius?

10. Who played Captain John H. Miller in the 1998 film 'Saving Private Ryan'?

ANSWERS:

1. Beef

2. Cheddar Gorge

3. Mount Olympus

4. Women's Institute

5. USA

6. 2

7. General Pinochet

8. John

9. Coin

10. Tom Hanks

TOM, DICK OR HARRY

1. Which English artist painted "Peasant Girl Gathering Sticks" in 1782?

2. Which Prime Minister announced the Open University in 1963 as a "University of the air"?

3. Who was the singer with The Verve?

4. Who was the subject of the play "A Man for All Seasons"?

5. Who defeated George McGovern and Hubert Humphrey in US Presidential elections?

6. Which American wrote this first novel "Never Love a Stranger" in 1948?

7. Which actor played Dr Gordon Thorpe in the sitcom "Only When I Laugh"?

8. With whom would you associate The Bluenotes?

9. Who built the Caledonian Canal?

10. Who wrote the 2002 autobiography "Losing My Virginity"?

ANSWERS:

1. Thomas Gainsborough

2. Harold Wilson

3. Richard Ashcroft

4. Thomas More

5. Richard Nixon

6. Harold Robbins

7. Richard Wilson

8. Harold Melvin

9. Thomas Telford

10. Richard Branson

FILMS 01

1. Who won a BAFTA award for leading actor in 1993 for the film "The Remains of the Day"?

2. Which actor starred in the 2005 remake of "War of the Worlds"?

3. Which actor starred in the 2000 film "Gladiator"?

4. Which actress starred in the 1994 film "Corrina Corrina"?

5. Vivian Ward and Edward Lewis were the central characters in which 1990 film?

6. The character Dr Emmett Brown featured in which series of movies?

7. Which 1975 movie starred Roy Scheider, Robert Shaw and Richard Dreyfuss?

8. Which city is the setting for the 1995 film "Casino"?

9. Which actress starred in the 1999 film "You've Got Mail"?

10. Chico, Grouch and Harpo formed which comedy team?

ANSWERS:

1. Anthony Hopkins

2. Tom Cruise

3. Russell Crowe

4. Whoopi Goldberg

5. "Pretty Woman"

6. "Back to the Future"

7. "Jaws"

8. Las Vegas

9. Meg Ryan

10. Marx Brothers

E's ARE GOOD

1. What is a young eagle called?

2. What was the name of the donkey in the "Winnie the Pooh" books?

3. What portable toilet was invented in 1924 by chemical manufacturer Ephraim Louis Jackson?

4. Where was the Temple of Diana, one of the Seven Wonders of the World?

5. What was the name of the woman loved by "The Hunchback of Notre Dame"?

6. Which missile takes its name from the French for 'flying fish'?

7. Which part of the body is affected by Otitis Media an infection that is most common in young children?

8. What island was the reception centre for European immigrants to America from 1892 to 1943?

9. What is the name of the statuette awarded by the American Academy of Television Arts and Sciences?

10. Which No 1 hit for the Shamen contained the lyric "E's are good"?

ANSWERS:

1. Eaglet

2. Eeyore

3. Elsan

4. Ephesus

5. Esmeralda

6. Exocet

7. Ear

8. Ellis Island

9. Emmy

10. "Ebeneezer Goode"

TAKE A CHANCE 19

In this round each correct answer is worth 2 points making a possible score of 20. However if you get any question wrong your score for this round is halved. If you are not sure, leave an answer blank and you still score 2 points for each correct answer (unless you get one wrong!)

1. Which famous doll was created by Ruth Handler?

2. Which singer was known as 'The Walrus of Love'?

3. Which scientist won her second Nobel Prize in 1911?

4. The murderer 'Son of Sam' terrorised which American city in the 1970's?

5. Which famous Italian tenor always had a bent nail in his top pocket when he performed as a lucky charm?

6. Which country's basketball team refused to collect their silver medals after losing to the Soviet Union in the 1972 Olympic Final?

7. Which politician described the Millennium Dome as "a triumph of confidence over cynicism"?

8. "The Perils of Penelope Pitstop" was a spin-off from which TV show?

9. Which record producer, famous for his 'Wall of Sound', once held a gun to Leonard Cohen's head to achieve the vocal performance he was looking for?

10. Which bank robbers were gunned down in their car in Louisiana while they were enjoying bacon and tomato sandwiches?

ANSWERS:

1. Barbie
2. Barry White
3. Marie Curie
4. New York
5. Luciano Pavarotti
6. USA
7. Tony Blair
8. "Wacky Races"
9. Phil Spector
10. Bonnie & Clyde

POT LUCK 20

1. What is prepared in a tannery?

2. Through which process do plants produce glucose?

3. In which children's story does an unattractive bird become a swan?

4. In which month does the Queen officially celebrate her birthday?

5. In literature, Huckleberry Finn escapes from his father by sailing down which river?

6. During which World War did the Battle of Jutland take place?

7. Which South African athlete, famous for running barefoot, represented Great Britain in the 1984 Olympics?

8. What is the U.K telephone dialling code for Edinburgh?

9. How many stripes are there in total on the flag of the United States of America?

10. What does the musical instruction 'forte' mean?

ANSWERS:

1. Leather

2. Photosynthesis

3. "The Ugly Duckling"

4. June

5. Mississippi

6. WW I

7. Zola Budd

8. 0131

9. Thirteen

10. Loud

MONTHS

1. Which group had a top 10 hit in 1987 with "April Skies"?

2. With which TV series would you associate the character Sergeant June Ackland?

3. Who was murdered on the Ides of March in 44BC?

4. August Darnell is the real name of which singer?

5. Which group had a top 5 hit in 1992 with "November Rain"?

6. Who wrote the novel "The Hunt for Red October"?

7. Which city takes its name from the Portuguese for River of January?

8. Which group had a top 3 hit in 1978 with "September"?

9. Who directed the film "Born on the Fourth of July"?

10. Which group's only UK No 1 was "December '63 (Oh What a Night)" which reached the top in 1976?

ANSWERS:

1. Jesus & Mary Chain

2. "The Bill"

3. Julius Caesar

4. Kid Creole

5. Guns 'n' Roses

6. Tom Clancy

7. Rio de Janeiro

8. Earth, Wind & Fire

9. Oliver Stone

10. Four Seasons

EUROVISION SONG CONTEST

1. Nicole won the 1982 Eurovision Song Contest representing which country?

2. Which singer represented the United Kingdom in 1996 with "Ooh..Aah..Just A Little Bit"?

3. Which singer finished second in 1993 representing the UK with the song "Better the Devil You Know"?

4. Which British singer has finished second and third in the Eurovision Song Contest?

5. Which British singer tied for first place in 1969?

6. Which group won the 1997 Eurovision Song Contest representing the United Kingdom?

7. Which country has won the Eurovision Song Contest the most times?

8. Who sang Switzerland's winning song in 1988?

9. Who in 1967 became the first British winner?

10. Rosemary Brown was the real name of which Irish Eurovision Song Contest winner?

ANSWERS:

1. Germany

2. Gina G

3. Sonia

4. Cliff Richard

5. Lulu

6. Katrina and the Waves

7. Ireland (7)

8. Celine Dion ("Ne Partez pas sans Moi")

9. Sandie Shaw

10. Dana

FLOWERS (Chelsea Flower Show)

1. Who wrote the poem "Daffodils"?

2. Which actress starred in the film "Driving Miss Daisy"?

3. Which group topped the singles charts in 1969 with "Lily The Pink"?

4. Which US State, beginning with the letter M, is called the "Magnolia State"?

5. Which artist painted "Sunflowers"?

6. Which character in "Coronation Street" was played by Violet Carson?

7. Which former "Dr Who" was the star of the 1989/90 TV series "Campion"?

8. Which female American artist painted "Black Iris" in 1906 and many other pictures of flowers?

9. According to the song title, where were Max Bygraves' tulips from?

10. Which actress starred in the 1979 film "The Rose"?

ANSWERS:

1. William Wordsworth

2. Jessica Tandy

3. Scaffold

4. Mississippi

5. Vincent Van Gogh

6. Ena Sharples

7. Peter Davison

8. Georgia O'Keefe

9. Amsterdam

10. Bette Midler

TAKE A CHANCE 20

In this round each correct answer is worth 2 points making a possible score of 20. However if you get any question wrong your score for this round is halved. If you are not sure, leave an answer blank and you still score 2 points for each correct answer (unless you get one wrong!)

1. How many are there in a Baker's Dozen?

2. Who was the only post-war leader of the Labour Party not to contest a General Election in that post?

3. Which actress played a 14-year-old girl who witnesses the death of her father in the 1971 film "Walkabout"?

4. Paul Weller and Mick Talbot formed which pop duo?

5. Who was Prime Minister during the first Gulf War?

6. Which famous author lectured against slavery in the United States and toured Italy with companions Augustus Egg and Wilkie Collins?

7. Which 11-year-old became the youngest chess player to qualify for the national championships in 1977?

8. Who is the only left handed golfer to have won the US Masters on two occasions?

9. Which England cricketer appeared in adverts for Brylcreem in the 1950's?

10. Who was frequently described on "Shooting Stars" as a 50's throwback?

ANSWERS:

1. 13
2. John Smith
3. Jenny Agutter
4. Style Council
5. John Major
6. Charles Dickens
7. Nigel Short
8. Phil Mickelson
9. Denis Compton
10. Mark Lamarr

JUNE

POT LUCK 21

1. Coconuts grow on what kind of tree?

2. What instrument does Captain Corelli play in the novel by Louis de Bernieres?

3. What rank of clergyman is in charge of a diocese?

4. According to legend, St Patrick is supposed to have driven which animal out of Ireland?

5. In the 1982 film "E.T.", what is the name of the boy who finds and befriends the stranded alien?

6. The carpal bones are found in which part of the human body?

7. What was Britain's first space rocket called?

8. Which British film company used the symbol of a man striking a gong at the start of its features?

9. Kenneth Starr was the special prosecutor who investigated President Clinton's relationship with whom?

10. Excluding jokers, how many face cards are there in a standard 52 card pack?

ANSWERS:

1. Palm Tree

2. Mandolin

3. Bishop

4. Snakes

5. Elliott

6. Wrist

7. Blue Streak

8. Rank

9. Monica Lewinsky

10. 12

A NICE EASY ROUND

1. In which imaginary county is "Trumpton"?

2. Who launched the liner Queen Mary?

3. What is the middle name of Homer J. Simpson?

4. What was the name of the Tennessee hotel where Maxwell House coffee was first tested?

5. Where in Italy was Leonardo da Vinci born?

6. Where do the "Teletubbies" live?

7. Zurich is situated on the shores of which lake?

8. Where is Saint Edmund buried?

9. Who presented "Late Night Currie" on Radio 5 Live at the weekends from 1998 to 2003?

10. What was the first name of Dutch artist Rembrandt?

ANSWERS:

1. Trumptonshire

2. Queen Mary

3. Jay

4. Maxwell House

5. Vinci

6. Tellytubbyland

7. Lake Zurich

8. Bury St. Edmunds

9. Edwina Currie

10. Rembrandt (van Rijn)

DOMESTIC SCIENCE

1. Who was the presenter of "Ready Steady Cook" before Ainsley Harriott?

2. What colour is the neutral wire in domestic appliances?

3. Which spice comes from the dried stigma of a species of crocus?

4. Fusili, Linguine, Penne & Rigatoni are all varieties of what?

5. What type of meat is Pastrami?

6. Which TV cook is also a director of Norwich City Football Club?

7. What is the function of a ball cock in the home?

8. In French cuisine, a narrow strip of what is deep-fried to make a goujon?

9. Blanket, Chain, Feather and Cross are all types of what?

10. Who was the DIY "man who can" on BBC's "Changing Rooms"?

ANSWERS:

1. Fern Britton

2. Blue

3. Saffron

4. Pasta

5. Beef

6. Delia Smith

7. Regulates the level of water in a tank

8. Fish (Sole)

9. Stitch

10. Handy Andy (Andy Kane)

ALBUMS 01

1. Which Oasis album reportedly sold 350,000 copies in 7 days in 1995?

2. Whose 1975 album was entitled "Captain Fantastic and the Brown Dirt Cowboy"?

3. "Paranoid Android" was a hit single from which Radiohead album?

4. What was Michael Jackson's biggest selling album in the UK?

5. Who was the narrator on the 1978 album "War of the Worlds"?

6. Which 1986 Bon Jovi album sold over 17 million copies worldwide?

7. Whose 1992 "Unplugged" album won 6 Grammys, sold 7 million copies and featured the song "Tears in Heaven"?

8. The picture of a baby swimming after a dollar bill was recreated with the same boy in 2002 to mark the 10th anniversary of which group's album "Nevermind"?

9. Which 60's star made her comeback album "Broken English" in 1979?

10. Which Scottish band won the 2004 Mercury Music Prize with their self-titled debut album?

ANSWERS:

1. "(What's the Story) Morning Glory"

2. Elton John

3. "OK Computer"

4. "Bad" (3.9 million; Thriller 3.3 million)

5. Richard Burton

6. "Slippery When Wet"

7. Eric Clapton

8. Nirvana

9. Marianne Faithful

10. Franz Ferdinand

TAKE A CHANCE 21

In this round each correct answer is worth 2 points making a possible score of 20. However if you get any question wrong your score for this round is halved. If you are not sure, leave an answer blank and you still score 2 points for each correct answer (unless you get one wrong!)

1. Teal and Navy are shades of which colour?

2. What is the official name of MI5?

3. Which author created the private eye Sam Spade in 1930?

4. Which musician, who composed "The Entertainer", was called 'The Father of Ragtime'?

5. Which actor played the title role in the TV series "Boon"?

6. Which goalkeeper made his only World Cup appearance for England in the quarter-final against West Germany in 1970, his last game for his country?

7. Which Beatles chart topper does not feature its titles in its lyrics?

8. Who was the unrivalled queen of swinging London creating the 'Chelsea Girl' look?

9. In which 1979 film did Jane Fonda play a TV reporter present at a nuclear power plant when a meltdown is narrowly averted?

10. Which country music singer said, "It takes a lot of money to look this cheap"?

ANSWERS:

1. Blue

2. Security Service

3. Dashiell Hammett

4. Scott Joplin

5. Michael Elphick

6. Peter Bonetti

7. "The Ballad of John & Yoko"

8. Mary Quant

9. "The China Syndrome"

10. Dolly Parton

POT LUCK 22

1. What is the 'Charleston'?
2. In which city is the famous 'Via Dolorosa'?
3. In the 1993 film 'The Remains of the Day' what job does Anthony Hopkins character have?
4. The adjective 'pulmonary' refers to which organ in the body?
5. Open Sesame' is a line from which of the Arabian Nights stories?
6. Which British city's cathedral features a huge tapestry by Graham Sutherland?
7. Which British Explorer landed at Botany Bay in 1770?
8. What is the official language of the Canary Islands?
9. Which edible paper is made from the pith of an Asiatic tree?
10. Which rock group appeared in and played the music for the film 'Tommy'?

ANSWERS:

1. A Dance
2. Jerusalem
3. Butler
4. Lungs
5. "Ali Baba & the Forty Thieves"
6. Coventry
7. Captain James Cook
8. Spanish
9. Rice Paper
10. The Who

AFRICA

1. Who met whom at Ujiji in 1871?

2. Who starred in the 1973 film "Shaft in Africa"?

3. What is the second largest desert in Africa?

4. Who took the song "Africa" to No 3 in 1983?

5. Northern Rhodesia is now known as what?

6. Who wrote the novel "The African Queen"?

7. Which Moroccan city has a red hat named after it?

8. Which comedy duo starred in the films "The Road to Morocco" and "The Road to Zanzibar"?

9. What is the second longest river in Africa?

10. Which British Prime Minister famously said in Cape Town 1960, "the winds of change are blowing through this continent"?

ANSWERS:

1. Stanley met Livingston

2. Richard Roundtree

3. Kalahari

4. Toto

5. Zambia

6. C S Forrester

7. Fez

8. Bob Hope & Bing Crosby

9. River Congo (also Zaire)

10. Harold Macmillan

BLACK & BLUE

1. Who wrote "Black Beauty"?

2. In the University Boat Race, who are the Dark Blues?

3. From which country did the Black-Eyed Bean originate?

4. Who had a No 1 hit in 1986 with "True Blue"?

5. According to the nursery rhyme, how many blackbirds were baked into a pie?

6. What were Laurel & Hardy on the trail of in the Blue Ridge Mountains of Virginia?

7. What was the name of Honor Blackman's character in "Goldfinger"?

8. What type of food was Blue Vinny?

9. What was Black Lace's highest charting single in the UK reaching No. 2 in 1984?

10. Which city in the Sudan is at the confluence of the Blue Nile and the White Nile?

ANSWERS:

1. Anna Sewell

2. Oxford

3. China

4. Madonna

5. 24 (Four and Twenty)

6. The Lonesome Pine

7. Pussy Galore

8. Cheese

9. "Agadoo"

10. Khartoum

A LITTLE NIGHT MUSIC

1. Which American band charted in 1993 with "The Sidewinder Sleeps Tonite" and "Nightswimming"?

2. Who had a Top 20 hit in 1981 with "A Rainy Night in Georgia"?

3. Which musical features the song "The Music of the Night"?

4. According to the 1984 song from the musical "Chess", where did Murray Head spend "One Night"?

5. Who had a Top 10 hit in 1971 with "The Night They Drove Old Dixie Down"?

6. "I Could Have Danced All Night" featured in which musical?

7. Which girl group had a hit album and hit single titled "Ladies Night" in 2003?

8. Who had a No 1 hit in 1992 with "Goodnight Girl"?

9. "All Night Long (All Night)" was a UK No 2 in 1983 for which American singer?

10. For which Bond film did Gladys Knight sing the theme?

ANSWERS:

1. REM

2. Randy Crawford

3. "Phantom of the Opera"

4. Bangkok

5. Joan Baez

6. "My Fair Lady"

7. Atomic Kitten

8. Wet Wet Wet

9. Lionel Richie

10. "A Licence to Kill"

TAKE A CHANCE 22

In this round each correct answer is worth 2 points making a possible score of 20. However if you get any question wrong your score for this round is halved. If you are not sure, leave an answer blank and you still score 2 points for each correct answer (unless you get one wrong!)

1. Portrayed by Paul O'Grady, who was known as the 'Birkenhead Bombshell'?

2. Which actor played Han Solo in "Star Wars"?

3. Which British supermodel once said, "I make a lot of money, but I don't want to talk about that. I work very hard and I'm worth every cent"?

4. On which island was "Bergerac" set?

5. Which country music singer joined Sheena Easton on the hit duet "We've Got Tonight"?

6. What is the world's second largest fast food restaurant chain?

7. When asked by David Frost how he would describe himself, which member of the Royal Family replied, "Sometimes as a bit of a twit"?

8. Which civil rights leader first achieved national renown when he helped mobilise the black boycott of the Montgomery bus system in 1955?

9. Who married Texan librarian Laura Welch in 1977?

10. When England defeated Malta 5 – 0 at Wembley in May 1971, which goalkeeper touched the ball only 4 times, all from back passes and didn't have a save to make?

ANSWERS:

1. Lily Savage
2. Harrison Ford
3. Naomi Campbell
4. Jersey
5. Kenny Rogers
6. Burger King
7. Prince Charles
8. Martin Luther King
9. George W Bush
10. Gordon Banks

POT LUCK 23

1. Lourdes is a place of pilgrimage in which country?

2. In computer games what kind of animal is 'Sonic'?

3. Who did Prince Andrew marry in July 1986?

4. Which UK radio station transmits 'Woman's Hour'?

5. Which spirit is the essential ingredient of the cocktail, Planter's Punch?

6. What was the middle name of polar explorer Captain Robert Scott?

7. Barbara Woodhouse was mainly associated with training which animals?

8. Which football club are nicknamed the 'Shrimpers'?

9. Which comic book hero is the best-known creation of Joe Shuster and Jerry Siegel?

10. Which city is the capital of the US state of Hawaii?

ANSWERS:

1. France

2. Hedgehog

3. Sarah Fergusson

4. Radio 4

5. Rum

6. Falcon

7. Dogs

8. Southend United

9. Superman

10. Honolulu

KID'S STUFF 01

1. What was the name of Fred Flintstone's best friend and neighbour?

2. In which fictional land does Noddy live?

3. Which cartoon character first appeared in the 1920s, and was accompanied on his adventures by his dog Snowy?

4. In the nursery rhyme 'Hickory Dickory Dock', which creature ran up the clock?

5. In the book 'Charlotte's Web', what type of animal was the character Wilbur?

6. The TV characters 'Po' and 'Dipsy' live in which imaginary land?

7. What was the name of the orange-faced people who worked in Willy Wonka's chocolate factory?

8. In the TV programme 'Tweenies', what is the name of the dog?

9. In the 'Toy Story' films, what is the name of the dinosaur?

10. Which famous US basketball star appeared alongside Bugs Bunny in the 1996 film 'Space Jam'?

ANSWERS:

1. Barney Rubble

2. Toyland

3. Tintin

4. Mouse

5. Pig

6. Tellytubby Land

7. Oompa Loompas

8. Doodles

9. Rex

10. Michael Jordan

INITIAL SUCCESS 03

The first letter of each answer to questions 1 – 9 spells out the name of a place. Question 10 relates to that place.

1. Which sitcom starred Paul Nicholas and Jan Francis?

2. Which suffragette was killed by the King's horse during the 1913 Derby?

3. Which tennis player won 3 of the 4 Grand Slam tournaments in 2004?

4. Which TV quiz was based upon the American show "College Bowl"?

5. Which actor returned to the role of James Bond in the film "Diamonds are Forever"?

6. Who was the youngest member of England's World Cup winning team in 1966?

7. Which group was formed by the runners-up in the TV series "Popstars"?

8. Which singer topped the charts in 2001 with "What Took You So Long"?

9. Which scientist won her second Nobel Prize in 1911?

10. This city is the capital of which country?

ANSWERS:

1. "Just Good Friends"
2. Emily Davidson
3. Roger Federer
4. "University Challenge"
5. Sean Connery
6. Alan Ball
7. Liberty X
8. Emma Bunton
9. Marie Curie
10. Israel

FICTIONAL DOCTORS

1. Which TV series features Hugh Quarshie as surgeon Ric Griffin?

2. What was the nickname of "Star Trek's" Doctor McCoy?

3. Who directed the 1963 film "Doctor Strangelove"?

4. Which of Hinge and Bracket was the doctor?

5. Who played Honey Ryder in the 1962 film "Dr No"?

6. Who metamorphoses into "The Incredible Hulk"?

7. What was the name of George Clooney's character in "ER"?

8. Who created the character Dr Jekyll?

9. Which ITV drama is set in the fictional West Country fishing village of Portwenn?

10. What was the first name of Dr Watson in the "Sherlock Holmes" stories?

ANSWERS:

1. "Holby City"

2. 'Bones'

3. Stanley Kubrick

4. Dr Evadne Hinge

5. Ursula Andress

6. Dr Bruce Banner

7. Dr Doug Ross

8. Robert Louis Stevenson

9. "Doc Martin"

10. John

TAKE A CHANCE 23

In this round each correct answer is worth 2 points making a possible score of 20. However if you get any question wrong your score for this round is halved. If you are not sure, leave an answer blank and you still score 2 points for each correct answer (unless you get one wrong!)

1. Which Prime Minister opened the M25 motorway in October 1986?

2. Which striker joined Everton from Leicester City for £800,000 in the summer of 1985?

3. In lonely hearts columns, what do the letters WTT stand for?

4. In which William Shakespeare play did Shylock appear?

5. In which TV series did Patrick Duffy play a character called Mark Harris?

6. Which former disc jockey recorded the song "Snot Rap"?

7. Which group were joined on hit singles by Chrissie Hynde and Robert Palmer?

8. Which type of underwear became popular after being worn in a TV advert by Nick Kamen?

9. Which playwright once said, "Bigamy is having one wife too many. Monogamy is the same"?

10. Who was mayor of London three times between 1397 and 1420?

ANSWERS:

1. Margaret Thatcher

2. Gary Lineker

3. Willing to Travel

4. "The Merchant of Venice"

5. "The Man from Atlantis"

6. Kenny Everett

7. UB40

8. Boxer Shorts

9. Oscar Wilde

10. Dick Whittington

POT LUCK 24

1. What is the longest river in South America?

2. Which metal was famously mined in Cornwall in the 19th century?

3. Which British prime minister introduced voting by secret ballot in 1872?

4. What does a notaphilist collect?

5. Which spa and resort in Derbyshire is famous for its mineral waters first used by the Romans?

6. If you had just sternutated, what would you have done?

7. How many British kings have been called George?

8. Checkpoint Charlie was a crossing point along which former east German landmark?

9. What was the real first name of Groucho Marx?

10. Which was the first programme transmitted when Channel 4 began in November 1982?

ANSWERS:

1. Amazon

2. Tin

3. William Gladstone

4. Bank Notes

5. Buxton

6. Sneezed

7. Six

8. Berlin Wall

9. Julius

10. "Countdown"

SUMMER

1. Which actress starred in the 1997 film "I Know What You Did Last Summer" and its 1998 sequel?

2. Who is the Queen of the Fairies in "A Midsummer Nights Dream"?

3. Which actor played Foggy Dewhurst in "Last of the Summer Wine"?

4. Which word can precede file, summer and ink?

5. Abba's hit "Summer Night City" is a tribute to which Swedish city?

6. Which American playwright wrote the plays "Summer and Smoke" in 1948 and "Suddenly Last Summer" in 1958?

7. Who has a summer residence at Castel Gandolfo?

8. Which is the only country to have hosted the Summer Olympic Games 4 times?

9. The song "Summer Nights" by John Travolta & Olivia Newton John is featured in which film?

10. Which group had top 10 hits in the 80's with "I Want You Back" and "Cruel Summer"?

ANSWERS:

1. Jennifer Love Hewitt

2. Titania

3. Brian Wilde

4. Indian

5. Stockholm

6. Tennessee Williams

7. The Pope

8. USA

9. "Grease"

10. Bananarama

FATHER'S DAY

1. Which singer had a hit with "Father Figure" in 1988?

2. Who created the priest detective Father Brown?

3. Which actor played Gerry Conlon in 1993 film "In The Name of the Father"?

4. Father Abraham was associated with which cartoon characters?

5. Which Greek physician was called 'The Father of Medicine'?

6. Which playwright said, "Land of my fathers? My fathers can have it"?

7. Which actor played the title role in the 1991 film "Father of the Bride"?

8. Who was the father of King Edward VII?

9. Who wrote the novel "Fatherland" in 1992?

10. Which group had a top 3 hit in 1995 with "Father & Son"

ANSWERS:

1. George Michael

2. G K Chesterton

3. Daniel Day-Lewis

4. The Smurfs

5. Hippocrates

6. Dylan Thomas

7. Steve Martin

8. Prince Albert

9. Robert Harris

10. Boyzone

FOOD

1. Which fruit sauce is traditionally served with turkey?

2. Americans call this vegetable zucchini, what do we call it?

3. Who wrote and starred in the TV sitcom "dinnerladies"?

4. In Scotland, what is a bridie?

5. In which country did the Granny Smith apple originate?

6. From which animal is brawn made?

7. What type of vegetable is a Webb's Wonder?

8. Who "dined on mince and slices of quince, which they ate with a runcible spoon"?

9. In which country did Piccalilli originate?

10. What was invented by Sir Marcus Sandys and first made by grocers Lea & Perrins?

ANSWERS:

1. Cranberry

2. Courgette

3. Victoria Wood

4. Meat Pasty/Pie

5. Australia

6. Pig

7. Lettuce

8. The Owl & The Pussycat

9. Britain

10. Worcestershire Sauce

TAKE A CHANCE 24

In this round each correct answer is worth 2 points making a possible score of 20. However if you get any question wrong your score for this round is halved. If you are not sure, leave an answer blank and you still score 2 points for each correct answer (unless you get one wrong!)

1. Who said, "If that's justice then I'm a banana" following a libel award against Private Eye magazine?

2. Which children's TV character lived at Colley's Mill?

3. Curly and Pieface are friends of which comic strip character?

4. Which author created the terms 'love letter' and 'elbow room'?

5. Indonesia and Zanzibar are chief sources of which aromatic cooking ingredient?

6. During WWI, which famous scientist helped to equip ambulances with X-ray equipment, which she drove to the front lines?

7. Which Disney film featured kittens called Toulouse, Marie and Berlioz?

8. What were black and later cherry red, popular with postmen and policemen and were then adopted by 'mods' in the mid 60's?

9. Which rock singer was nicknamed 'The Lizard King'?

10. After leaving the England job, both Kevin Keegan and Sven Goran Eriksson managed which Premiership club?

ANSWERS:

1. Ian Hislop

2. Windy Miller

3. Dennis the Menace

4. William Shakespeare

5. Cloves

6. Marie Curie

7. "The Aristocats"

8. Dr Martens

9. Jim Morrison

10. Manchester City

JULY

POT LUCK 25

1. With which roast meat is apple sauce traditionally served?

2. What present day country was the head of the Ottoman Empire?

3. A water moccasin is what type of creature?

4. What is the official language of Liechtenstein?

5. Which British city was nicknamed Cottonopolis?

6. Who was the Siberian mystic who had great influence over Czarina Alexandra and Czar Nicholas II?

7. Is a 'contralto' a male or female voice?

8. What colour was the adhesive one penny stamp first issued on 6th May 1840?

9. The term cardiac refers to which part of the human body?

10. Which famous bell was heard chiming in London for the first time in 1859?

ANSWERS:

1. Pork

2. Turkey

3. Snake

4. German

5. Manchester

6. Rasputin

7. Female

8. Black

9. Heart

10. Big Ben

CANADA (Canada Day – 1ˢᵗ July)

1. What is Canada's chief Pacific sea port?

2. What is the capital of Canada?

3. Which Canadian city hosted the 1976 Summer Olympic Games?

4. What is the official language of the Canadian province Quebec?

5. Which Canadian singer was the first to appear at the Live Aid concert in the United States?

6. Who was Prime Minister of Canada from 1968 to 1979 and from 1980 to 1984?

7. What is the national sport of Canada?

8. The Major League Baseball team the Blue Jays are from which city?

9. What is the national emblem of Canada?

10. London in Ontario, Canada is situated on which river?

ANSWERS:

1. Vancouver

2. Ottawa

3. Montreal

4. French

5. Bryan Adams

6. Pierre Trudeau

7. Lacrosse (Summer); Ice Hockey (Winter)

8. Toronto

9. Maple Leaf

10. Thames

TV 02

1. Which TV programme was presented by Stuart Hall and Eddie Wearing?

2. In which country was the TV series "Secret Army" set?

3. Which cartoon series featured Peter Perfect and Professor Pat Pending?

4. The TV series "Columbo" was set in which city?

5. Which 90's high-tech BBC TV series starred Craig McLachlan, Jaye Griffiths and Jesse Birdsall?

6. Which actress plays Susan Harper in the sitcom "My Family"?

7. Who is the presenter of "Strictly Dance Fever"?

8. Hannibal Hayes and Kid Curry were the central characters in which US TV series?

9. Who took over from Johnny Carson as the presenter of the "Tonight Show" in 1992?

10. Which TV series is set in Wisteria Lane?

ANSWERS:

1. "It's A Knockout"

2. Belgium

3. "Wacky Races"

4. Los Angeles

5. "Bugs"

6. Zoe Wanamaker

7. Graham Norton

8. "Alias Smith & Jones"

9. Jay Leno

10. "Desperate Housewives"

BORN IN THE USA (Independence Day 4th July)

1. Which US President said, "All free men…are citizens of Berlin"?
2. Which singer topped the charts in 1966 with "Strangers in the Night"?
3. Who won an Oscar for directing the film "Annie Hall"?
4. Who wrote the novel "A Farewell to Arms"?
5. Which basketball player won his 5th NBA MVP award in 1998?
6. Who wrote Diana Ross' hit single "Muscles"?
7. Which actor starred in the 1967 film "Cool Hand Luke"?
8. Which golfer won the 1997 US Masters by 12 strokes?
9. Who was the 43rd Vice President of the US who went on to become the 41st President in 1989?
10. Which singer recorded the album "Born in the USA"?

ANSWERS:

1. John F Kennedy
2. Frank Sinatra
3. Woody Allen
4. Ernest Hemingway
5. Michael Jordan
6. Michael Jackson
7. Paul Newman
8. Tiger Woods
9. George H W Bush (Senior)
10. Bruce Springsteen

TAKE A CHANCE 25

In this round each correct answer is worth 2 points making a possible score of 20. However if you get any question wrong your score for this round is halved. If you are not sure, leave an answer blank and you still score 2 points for each correct answer (unless you get one wrong!)

1. What do the initials DPC mean to a builder?

2. Which brand of tea has been advertised on TV by animals trained at Twycross Zoo?

3. Which of the Rolling Stones once said, "I only get ill when I give up drugs"?

4. Kim Basinger appeared in which James Bond film?

5. The singles finals at Wimbledon take place during which month?

6. Which "Coronation Street" character died of a heart attack following a road rage incident?

7. Which organisation's flag depicts a map of the world flanked by olive branches?

8. Which was the only act to perform at Woodstock, Live Aid and Live 8?

9. Which literary character invented a gobstopper that lasted forever?

10. What was famously found by a dog belonging to Thames river boat worker David Corbett?

ANSWERS:

1. Damp Proof Course
2. PG Tips
3. Keith Richards
4. "Never Say Never Again"
5. July
6. Derek Wilton
7. United Nations
8. The Who
9. Willy Wonka
10. World Cup (Jules Rimet Trophy)

POT LUCK 26

1. What is the hobby of a campanologist?

2. In 1919, John Alcock and Arthur Brown made the first non-stop flight across which ocean?

3. Pure gold consists of how many carats?

4. The wine, Bull's Blood, comes from which country?

5. The Nikkei Stock Average is a leading index of share prices in which country?

6. What type of paper, used for copying, was invented in 1806 in England by Ralph Wedgwood?

7. The BCG vaccine is given to protect against which disease?

8. Which former Labour party leader is buried on the Scottish island of Iona?

9. What would be your occupation if you were a member of ABTA?

10. The American World War II heavy bomber, the B-17, was popularly known as the 'Flying .. what'?

ANSWERS:

1. Bell Ringing

2. Atlantic

3. 24

4. Hungary

5. Japan

6. Carbon Paper

7. Tuberculosis

8. John Smith

9. Travel Agent

10. Fortress

FRANCE (Bastille Day)

1. Which French town, the site of the shrine to St Bernadette, has a reputation for miraculous cures?

2. Which French town is famous for its 24 hour motor race?

3. In which town was Joan of Arc burned at the stake?

4. What is the name of the marshy area in the Rhone delta famous for its horses?

5. The Tour de France ends in which city?

6. In which French city is the Council of Europe?

7. With which car company would you associate the Xantia?

8. What is the longest river in France?

9. Which town in Burgundy is famous for its mustard?

10. In which city were French Kings traditionally crowned?

ANSWERS:

1. Lourdes

2. Le Mans

3. Rouen

4. Camargue

5. Paris

6. Strasbourg

7. Citroen

8. Loire

9. Dijon

10. Rheims

ALBUMS 02

1. What was the title of Oasis's first album released in 1994?

2. Whose album "Life for Rent" was the biggest selling album in the UK in 2003?

3. Who "Revisited Highway 61" in 1965?

4. What was the Michael Jackson's follow up album to "Thriller" called?

5. "Synchronicity", released in 1983, was which band's last studio album?

6. Which pop group made a 2006 comeback with the No 1 album "Beautiful World"?

7. Who released the 1971 album "Every Picture Tells a Story", the first to simultaneously go to No 1 in both Britain and the US?

8. Which Eric Clapton album of 1977 shared its name with a pointer Sisters hit single?

9. What was the title of the Spice Girls first album?

10. "Meat is Murder" was a 1985 album from which miserable Mancunians?

ANSWERS:

1. "Definitely Maybe"

2. Dido

3. Bob Dylan

4. "Bad"

5. Police

6. Take That

7. Rod Stewart

8. "Slow Hand"

9. "Spice"

10. The Smiths

NUMBERS

1. How many is a score?

2. If you were celebrating your Pearl wedding anniversary, how many years would you have been married?

3. How many islands make up the Azores in the North Atlantic Ocean – 6, 9 or 12?

4. How many are there in a baker's dozen?

5. In bingo which number is Two Little Ducks?

6. How many players are there in a cricket team?

7. What was Patrick McGoohan's number in "The Prisoner"?

8. Which number would you associate with Dudley Moore and Bo Derek?

9. In the authorised version of the Bible, which number Psalm begins 'The Lord is my Shepherd'?

10. What is the maximum score that can be obtained with one dart?

ANSWERS:

1. 20

2. 30

3. 9

4. 13

5. 22

6. 11

7. 6

8. 10

9. 23

10. 60

TAKE A CHANCE 26

In this round each correct answer is worth 2 points making a possible score of 20. However if you get any question wrong your score for this round is halved. If you are not sure, leave an answer blank and you still score 2 points for each correct answer (unless you get one wrong!)

1. Shot dead in 1877, Frank Cahill was whose first victim?

2. Which famous boxer once said, "Your hands can't hit what your eyes can't see"?

3. What was the name of the vigilante organisation sponsored by Michael Winner to patrol the London Underground?

4. In which 1999 film did Julia Roberts suffer from an aversion to weddings?

5. In the novel "Peter Pan" what is the name of the Indian princes rescued by Peter?

6. Which actress plays the title character's Aunt Joan in the TV series "Doc Martin"?

7. Which museum, opened by King Edward VII in 1909, was named after his parents?

8. How many separate squares are there on a Rubik's Cube?

9. Which Canadian supermodel is known as 'The Chameleon'?

10. "It's a rich man's world" is the last line of which Abba hit?

ANSWERS:

1. Billy the Kid
2. Muhammad Ali
3. Guardian Angels
4. "Runaway Bride"
5. Tiger Lily
6. Stephanie Cole
7. Victoria & Albert Museum
8. 54
9. Linda Evangelista
10. "Money, Money, Money"

POT LUCK 27

1. The love-apple is an old name for which fruit?

2. Affiliated to the United Nations, in which country is the World Bank located?

3. Juan Peron was president of which country from 1946-1955 and again from 1973-1974?

4. In Rudyard Kipling's 'The Jungle Book', what kind of animal was the character 'Akela'?

5. What type of creature is a bustard?

6. The River Aire cuts a gap through which range of hills?

7. What is the main ingredient of a sauce soubise?

8. Which leader of Germany twice failed to gain entry to the Vienna Academy of Fine Arts, in the early 1900s?

9. In 'The Muppet Show', what was Miss Piggy's surname?

10. Frascati wine comes from hills near which Italian city?

ANSWERS:

1. Tomato

2. USA

3. Argentina

4. Wolf

5. Bird

6. Pennines

7. Onions

8. Adolf Hitler

9. Lee

10. Rome

THE HEAT IS ON

1. Glen Frey's hit "The Heat is On" was featured in which movie?

2. Which word can precede the words heat, centre and ringer?

3. The 1995 film "Heat" is set in which US city?

4. Johnnie & Keith Wilder were members of which 70's soul/disco group?

5. "They Call Me Mr Tibbs" was the sequel to which film?

6. Which US President said, "If you can't stand the heat, get out of the kitchen"?

7. Which actor starred in the 1949 film "White Heat"?

8. Who said of the possibility of reforming the Beatles, "You can't re-heat a soufflé"?

9. Which Commonwealth country provides the setting for the 1983 Merchant Ivory film "Heat & Dust"?

10. "Heatseeker" in 1988 was the highest charting single in the UK for which Australian rock band?

ANSWERS:

1. "Beverley Hills Cop"

2. Dead

3. Los Angeles

4. Heatwave

5. "In The Heat of the Night"

6. Harry Truman

7. James Cagney

8. Paul McCartney

9. India

10. AC/DC

SUMMER SPORT

1. Which golfer won his eighth European Order of Merit title in 2005?

2. Which American cyclist won his seventh Tour de France in 2005?

3. Which athlete won the Men's 110 metres Hurdles at the 1999 World Championships?

4. Which England bowler took 9 wickets in an innings against South Africa in 1994?

5. In which month is the Derby run?

6. Which tennis player won the 1976 Wimbledon Men's Singles title without dropping a set in the entire tournament?

7. Graham Gooch played cricket for which county?

8. Which baseball team play their home games at Fenway Park?

9. How many left-handed golfers have won any of the Major Championship titles?

10. Who in 1999 became only the fifth tennis player to win all 4 Men's 'Grand Slam' singles titles?

ANSWERS:

1. Colin Montgomerie

2. Lance Armstrong

3. Colin Jackson

4. Devon Malcolm

5. June

6. Bjorn Borg

7. Essex

8. Boston Red Sox

9. 3 (Bob Charles, Mike Weir & Phil Mickelson)

10. Andre Agassi

GEOGRAPHY 01

1. Which is the highest mountain in Greece?

2. If you travelled due south from Reykjavik, on which continent would you next strike land?

3. What is the Arabic word for desert?

4. Which US State is known as The Lone Star State?

5. The Khyber Pass connects Afghanistan to which other country?

6. Which EU country has the longest coastline?

7. Which of these European capital cities is furthest east – Athens, Belgrade, Helsinki or Warsaw?

8. Which US State has the largest population?

9. Which South American river has 2 capital cities on its banks?

10. Babylonia is now part of which modern day country?

ANSWERS:

1. Mount Olympus

2. Antarctica

3. Sahara (or sahrá)

4. Texas

5. Pakistan

6. Great Britain

7. Helsinki

8. California

9. River Plate

10. Iraq

TAKE A CHANCE 27

In this round each correct answer is worth 2 points making a possible score of 20. However if you get any question wrong your score for this round is halved. If you are not sure, leave an answer blank and you still score 2 points for each correct answer (unless you get one wrong!)

1. Famous for talking to the animals, which literary character owned a dog called Jip and a pig called Gub?

2. Who lit the eternal flame at the grave of John F Kennedy at Arlington National Cemetery?

3. Which darts world champion of the 1980's was nicknamed the 'Milky Bar Kid'?

4. Which French historical figure received visions from God, through which she helped inspire Charles VII's troops to retake most of his former territories?

5. Which singer is nicknamed 'The Groover from Vancouver'?

6. What is the national airline of Ireland?

7. Which Madonna hit was extensively featured in the film "Austin Powers: The Spy Who Shagged Me"?

8. Which 1881 Wild West incident has been the subject of 29 films?

9. Which famous former Page 3 girl once said, "I have 10 pairs of trainers, one for each day of the week"?

10. Which Kenny Everett character is remembered for unsuccessfully attempting to flip cigarettes into his mouth?

ANSWERS:

1. Dr Doolittle
2. Jackie Kennedy
3. Keith Deller
4. Joan of Arc
5. Bryan Adams
6. Aer Lingus
7. "Beautiful Stranger"
8. Gunfight at the OK Corral
9. Samantha Fox
10. Sid Snot

POT LUCK 28

1. Who was the British Prime Minister from 1970-1974?

2. In which part of the body is the bone known as the anvil?

3. What is the official currency of Australia?

4. The kumquat, a fruit resembling a very small orange, originated in which country?

5. Who, in 1969, said "Houston, Tranquillity Base here. The Eagle has landed"?

6. What is the sign of the zodiac of someone born on St Patrick's Day?

7. The De Montfort Hall is which city's main concert hall?

8. What is a female ferret called?

9. In which city are the Parliamentary constituencies of Heeley and Brightside?

10. Bred in Argentina, the falabella is the smallest breed of what?

ANSWERS:

1. Edward Heath

2. Ear

3. Australian Dollar

4. China

5. Neil Armstrong

6. Pisces

7. Jill

8. Adolf Hitler

9. Sheffield

10. Horse

SOMETHING FOR THE WEEKEND

1. The line "Friday night and the lights are low" is from which Abba hit?

2. Which Saturday morning TV show featured Zoe Ball and Jamie Theakston from 1996 to 1999?

3. What was the name of ITV's Saturday afternoon sports programme first broadcast in 1965?

4. In which city was "Saturday Night Fever" set?

5. Who had a UK Number 1 single in 1994 with "Saturday Night"?

6. The novel "Saturday Night and Sunday Morning" is set in which English, midlands city?

7. Which British band had a top 5 hit with "Sunday Morning Call" in 2000?

8. Which sport features in the 1999 film "Any Given Sunday"?

9. Who was the author of the 1999 book "Ground Force Weekend Workbook"?

10. Who was the presenter of the Channel 4 show "Something for the Weekend"? (1999 – 2000)

ANSWERS:

1. "Dancing Queen"

2. "Live & Kicking"

3. "World of Sport"

4. New York

5. Whigfield

6. Nottingham

7. Oasis

8. American Football

9. Alan Titchmarsh

10. Denise Van Outen

MOTOWN

1. Which group had Top 10 hits in 1970 with "I Want You Back" and "ABC"?

2. Which group had a No 1 hit in 1970 with "Tears of a Clown"?

3. Stevie Wonder's hit "Sir Duke" was a tribute to which musician?

4. Diana Ross sang with which 1960's group?

5. Who wrote the Commodores hit "Three Times a Lady"?

6. Which group was formed by siblings called Ronald, Rudolph & O'Kelly?

7. Who founded Motown in 1959 and was its head until selling the company in 1988?

8. Which singer had hit duets with Diana Ross, Tammi Terrell, Kim Weston & Mary Wells?

9. What was the title of the Four Tops 1966 No 1 hit?

10. Which singer was backed by the Vandellas?

ANSWERS:

1. Jackson Five

2. Smokey Robinson & the Miracles

3. Duke Ellington

4. Supremes

5. Lionel Richie

6. Isley Brothers

7. Berry Gordy Jr.

8. Marvin Gaye

9. "Reach Out I'll Be There"

10. Martha Reeves

MATHS

1. What number used to set former English cricket umpire David Shepherd to lifting his feet in an agitated manner?

2. Which is the only even prime number?

3. Whose theorem states that, "in a right angled triangle, the sum of the squares of the shorter sides is equal to the square of the hypotenuse"?

4. How many in a gross?

5. Which 19th Century mathematician built The Difference Engine, recognised as the first computer?

6. What nationality was mathematician and code breaker Alan Turing who was the subject of the 1996 TV drama "Breaking the Code"?

7. What is the name of the system used to calculate the score target in rain affected one day cricket matches?

8. The duodecimal counting system uses which number as its base?

9. Which branch of mathematics is concerned with the properties of space, usually in terms of 2 and 3 dimensional figures?

10. Who was nominated for an Oscar for his portrayal of mathematician John Nash in the 2001 film "A Beautiful Mind"?

ANSWERS:

1. 111 (and multiples)

2. 2

3. Pythagoras

4. 144

5. Charles Babbage

6. British

7. Duckworth Lewis

8. 12

9. Geometry

10. Russell Crowe

TAKE A CHANCE 28

In this round each correct answer is worth 2 points making a possible score of 20. However if you get any question wrong your score for this round is halved. If you are not sure, leave an answer blank and you still score 2 points for each correct answer (unless you get one wrong!)

1. In the lyrics of the song, who is introduced as the singer of "Sgt Pepper's Lonely Hearts Club Band"?

2. Who was originally the resident astrologer on BBC's "Breakfast Time" TV show?

3. Marble Arch is situated at the end of Edgware Road, Park Lane and which famous London thoroughfare?

4. "Kitten Kong" was a famous episode of which 1970's TV show?

5. Which city is the legislative capital of South Africa, where the National Parliament and many government offices are located?

6. Who was the first boxer to defeat Joe Frazier in a professional fight?

7. In the Wild West, who was killed by Jack McCall while playing cards?

8. In which game does Mario have to jump over barrels while climbing ladders up a crooked construction site to rescue his girlfriend Pauline?

9. Who drew the cartoons for the "Molesworth" series of books?

10. Which member of the Royal Family once asked a Scottish driving instructor, "How do you keep the natives off the booze long enough to get them to pass the test"?

ANSWERS:

1. Billy Shears
2. Russell Grant
3. Oxford Street
4. "The Goodies"
5. Cape Town
6. George Foreman
7. Wild Bill Hickok
8. Donkey Kong
9. Ronald Searle
10. Prince Phillip (Duke of Edinburgh)

AUGUST

POT LUCK 29

1. Which meat is spiced to make pastrami?

2. What is the term for a restaurant charge if you bring your own wine?

3. The Star of Africa and the Jubilee are types of which precious gemstone?

4. Which British coin are there most of in circulation?

5. Which rodent was the original meat in a Brunswick stew, a traditional dish from the southeastern USA?

6. Ping pong is another name for which game?

7. Who was the archbishop of Cape Town between 1986 and 1996?

8. The names of how many US states contain the word New?

9. Which hilly area in northern England was designated the UK's first national park in 1951?

10. Created by Raymond Briggs which fictional character has a wife called Mildew?

ANSWERS:

1. Beef

2. Corkage

3. Diamonds

4. Penny

5. Squirrel

6. Table Tennis

7. Desmond Tutu

8. 4

9. Peak District

10. Fungus the Bogeyman

TV SOAPS

1. Which "EastEnders" baddie was played by John Altman?

2. Which actress played Krystle Carrington in "Dynasty"?

3. Which character in "Neighbours" is played by Stefan Dennis?

4. In "Brookside" what was the nickname of Thomas Sweeney?

5. In which English city is "Hollyoaks" set?

6. Which actor played teacher Grant Mitchell in "Home & Away"?

7. Which soap opera was launched with the promotion "sun, sangria and sex"?

8. In "Coronation Street" what role is played by Beverley Callard?

9. What was the original name of the village in "Emmerdale Farm"?

10. Which character in "Dallas" was played by Priscilla Presley?

ANSWERS:

1. Nick Cotton

2. Linda Evans

3. Paul Robinson

4. Sinbad

5. Chester

6. Craig McLachlan

7. "Eldorado"

8. Liz McDonald

9. Beckindale

10. Jenna Wade

NUMBER ONES

1. Which group recorded "World in Motion" with the 1990 England World Cup squad?

2. Who had a number one hit in 2004 with "Mysterious Girl"?

3. Which UK No. 1 hit also won an Oscar for the 1984 film "The Woman in Red"?

4. Which group had a UK No.1 with "21 Seconds" in 2001?

5. Which singer had a number one hit with "It's Not Unusual"?

6. Which singer appeared with Take That on the hit "Relight My Fire"?

7. Which singer's first No. 1 single was "I'm the Leader of the Gang (I Am)"?

8. Which Blur single entered the charts at No. 1 in 1995, just beating Oasis to the top spot?

9. Whose first UK No. 1 was "The Real Slim Shady" in 2000?

10. Who was the first (and also the last) of the Beatles to have a solo No. 1 single in the British charts?

ANSWERS:

1. New Order

2. Peter Andre

3. "I Just Called to Say I Love You"

4. So Solid Crew

5. Tom Jones

6. Lulu

7. Gary Glitter

8. "Country House"

9. Eminem

10. George Harrison

BRITISH CITIES

1. In which city is the Palace of Holyrood House?

2. Which English city has Football League clubs called City and Rovers?

3. In which city was "The Full Monty" set?

4. Which city is served by Aldergrove Airport?

5. The 1970's game show "Sale of the Century" was broadcast from which city?

6. Which British city failed in its bid to host the 2000 Olympic Games?

7. In which Scottish city is the Albert Institute and Caird Hall?

8. In which city is the DVLA based?

9. The pop group The Specials were formed in which city?

10. In which city is Aintree racecourse?

ANSWERS:

1. Edinburgh

2. Bristol

3. Sheffield

4. Belfast

5. Norwich

6. Manchester

7. Dundee

8. Swansea

9. Coventry

10. Liverpool

TAKE A CHANCE 29

In this round each correct answer is worth 2 points making a possible score of 20. However if you get any question wrong your score for this round is halved. If you are not sure, leave an answer blank and you still score 2 points for each correct answer (unless you get one wrong!)

1. Which Italian city is called 'The Queen of the Adriatic'?

2. In the USA they are called pantyhose, what are they called in the UK?

3. Which number is represented by the Roman numeral M?

4. Who was the Deputy Chief Constable of Greater Manchester cleared of misconduct following allegations that he was associating with criminals in 1986?

5. Who was nominated for Best Actor Oscars in the 1970's for his roles in the films "And Justice for All" and "The Godfather, Part II"?

6. Who was born on 4th August 1821, died on 27th February 1892 and designed and manufactured luggage in Paris during the second half of the 19th century?

7. Which England goalkeeper kept 6 clean sheets in his nine appearances at the World Cup finals?

8. What is the highest capital city in the world?

9. Which Beatles song spent 9 weeks at No 1 in the US charts?

10. Which former female newsreader now has a company that designs socks?

ANSWERS:
1. Venice
2. Tights
3. 1000
4. John Stalker
5. Al Pacino
6. Louis Vuitton
7. Gordon Banks
8. La Paz
9. "Hey Jude"
10. Selina Scott

POT LUCK 30

1. Who died in Spandau Prison in August 1987?

2. Which reggae singer inspired Stevie Wonder's hit "Masterblaster (Jammin')"?

3. In which US state is the city of Boston?

4. What is the home town of "Bob the Builder"?

5. Which film director, the son of a greengrocer in Leytonstone, died in 1980 aged 80?

6. Which children's TV show was set inside Sir Basil and Lady Rosemary's walled garden?

7. In which 1989 film did Beau and Jeff Bridges play brothers called Jack and Frank?

8. Which politician, in 1987, denied having a homosexual affair with Norman Scott?

9. What is the name of a dessert consisting of ice cream, fruit and cream served in a tall glass?

10. Which rock legend first burnt his guitar on stage at the Finsbury Park Astoria in March 1967, turning it into a regular practice at the end of his concerts?

ANSWERS:

1. Rudolf Hess

2. Bob Marley

3. Massachusetts

4. Bobsville

5. Alfred Hitchcock

6. "The Herbs"

7. "The Fabulous Baker Boys"

8. Jeremy Thorpe

9. Knickerbocker Glory

10. Jimi Hendrix

FAMOUS WOMEN

1. Media mogul Ted Turner was the 3rd husband of which Oscar winning actress?

2. Who wrote the novel "Death of an Expert Witness" which features detective Adam Dalgleish?

3. Which singer recorded "World in Union" the theme to the 1991 Rugby World Cup?

4. Which actress once said, "Its better to be looked over than to be overlooked"?

5. Which singer recorded "No Angel" the biggest selling British album of 2001?

6. Whose memoirs were entitled "The Downing Street Years"?

7. Which tennis player won her sixth consecutive Wimbledon Ladies Singles title in 1987?

8. Who was declared the sexiest woman of the century by Playboy in 1998?

9. Whose 1980's series was sub-titled "As Seen on TV"?

10. Which supermodel appeared with Michael Jackson on the video for the song "In The Closet"?

ANSWERS:

1. Jane Fonda

2. PD James

3. Kiri Te Kanawa

4. Mae West

5. Dido

6. Margaret Thatcher

7. Martina Navratilova

8. Marilyn Monroe

9. Victoria Wood

10. Naomi Campbell

FRUITY

1. The flavoured brandy kirsch is made using which fruit?

2. Which 15th century explorer brought the pineapple, a native of South America, to Spain?

3. Which American singer had a hit with "Blueberry Hill" in 1956?

4. The Phantom Raspberry Blower of Old London Town featured in which TV show?

5. What colour are limes when fully ripe?

6. In which country was the Loganberry developed in 1881 by James H Logan?

7. Viticulture is the name given to the growing of which fruit?

8. Which country produces the most apples – China, France, South Africa or USA?

9. Who wrote "James and the Giant Peach"?

10. Most of the world's production of which berry comes from just 37,000 acres in 5 US States?

ANSWERS:

1. Cherries

2. Christopher Columbus

3. Fats Domino

4. "The Two Ronnies"

5. Yellow

6. United States of America

7. Grapes

8. China (41%)

9. Roald Dahl

10. Cranberry

INITIAL SUCCESS 04

The first letter of each answer to questions 1 – 9 spells out the name of a TV programme. Question 10 relates to that TV programme.

1. What disease was previously called consumption?

2. Which actor won an Oscar for his performance in the film "The African Queen"?

3. What type of animal is the popular French children's fictional character Babar?

4. Peters & Lee and Lena Zavaroni were discovered on which TV talent show?

5. What is an official language of Haiti despite being spoken by only 10% of the population?

6. Which controversial 80's band took their name from an old headline about Frank Sinatra's film plans?

7. What is Elvis Presley's best selling single in the UK?

8. Which famous ship has been on display at Greenwich since 1957?

9. What was the name of the boy played by Henry Thomas in the film "ET"?

10. Which song was the theme to this TV series?

ANSWERS:

1. Tuberculosis

2. Humphrey Bogart

3. Elephant

4. "Opportunity Knocks"

5. French

6. Frankie Goes to Hollywood

7. "It's Now or Never"

8. Cutty Sark

9. Elliott

10. "Handbags & Gladrags"

TAKE A CHANCE 30

In this round each correct answer is worth 2 points making a possible score of 20. However if you get any question wrong your score for this round is halved. If you are not sure, leave an answer blank and you still score 2 points for each correct answer (unless you get one wrong!)

1. In which city is Hollywood Boulevard?

2. Who wrote the music for "Jesus Christ Superstar"?

3. Which organisation manages the UK's foreign exchange and gold reserves?

4. The video for which of her No 1 singles saw Kylie Minogue wearing revealing gold hot pants?

5. Which character in "101 Dalmatians" has a country house nicknamed 'Hell Hall'?

6. Who wrote "The Hitchhiker's Guide to the Galaxy"?

7. Who worked as a psychiatric nurse until the mid 80's, when she was persuaded by agent Malcolm Hardes to begin a career in stand-up comedy?

8. Which San Francisco 49ers player won his 3rd Super Bowl MVP award in 1990?

9. Which character in "Dad's Army" frequently threatened to set his mother on Captain Mainwaring after being told off?

10. Jordan has described which model's nose as resembling "a builder's elbow" and likened her breasts to a spaniel's ears?

ANSWERS:

1. Los Angeles
2. Andrew Lloyd Webber
3. Bank of England
4. "Spinning Around"
5. Cruella de Vil
6. Douglas Adams
7. Jo Brand
8. Joe Montana
9. Private Pike
10. Jodie Marsh

POT LUCK 31

1. Tewkesbury is a market town in which county?

2. "The Remorseful Day" was the last novel featuring which fictional police inspector?

3. What in Russia is a samovar?

4. In economics, what do the initials R.P.I stand for?

5. What was the title of the second 'Dirty Harry' film?

6. In which decade was the first Edinburgh Festival?

7. During which war did astronaut Buzz Aldrin serve as a US Airforce Pilot?

8. What is the smallest number of coins needed to make a total of one pound sixty-five pence?

9. What is the first event in an Olympic decathlon?

10. In which city are there roads called Goose Gate and Maid Marian Way?

ANSWERS:

1. Gloucestershire

2. Inspector Morse

3. Tea Urn

4. Retail Price Index

5. "Magnum Force"

6. 1940's (1947)

7. Korean

8. 4

9. 100 metres

10. Nottingham

SPORTING STARS

1. Which boxer beat Kostya Tszyu to win the IBF World Light Welterweight title in 2004?

2. Which British athlete won the Decathlon gold medal at the 1980 and 1984 Olympic Games?

3. Who was the IRB International Player of the Year for 2003?

4. Which tennis player won his third consecutive Wimbledon Men's Singles title in 1995?

5. Which goalkeeper appeared in his $1,000^{th}$ League match in December 1996?

6. Which cricketer hit a record 80 sixes in first class cricket during the 1985 season?

7. Who was the last golfer to retain his British Open Championship title?

8. Who won his first World Professional Snooker title in 1990?

9. Who became the first jockey to ride 2000 winners in National Hunt Racing?

10. Who in 1986 became the first driver for 26 years to retain his Formula 1 World Championship?

ANSWERS:

1. Ricky Hatton

2. Daley Thompson

3. Jonny Wilkinson

4. Pete Sampras

5. Peter Shilton

6. Ian Botham

7. Tiger Woods (2005 & 2006)

8. Stephen Hendry

9. Tony McCoy

10. Alain Prost

GEOGRAPHY 02

1. In which country is Andalusia?

2. In which sea is the island of Cuba?

3. The Galapagos Islands belong to which country?

4. In which country is the Great Dividing Range?

5. Ankara is the capital of which country?

6. Which is the only country to share a border with Denmark?

7. In which mountain range is Mount Everest?

8. What is the world's largest freshwater lake?

9. In which country is the city of Johannesburg?

10. The River Thames flows into which sea?

ANSWERS:

1. Spain

2. Caribbean

3. Ecuador

4. Australia

5. Turkey

6. Germany

7. Himalayas

8. Lake Superior

9. South Africa

10. North Sea

FILMS 02

1. Who played Dr. Alan Grant in "Jurassic Park 3"?

2. Which 1989 comedy featured John Travolta, Kirstie Alley and a talkative baby?

3. What was the name of the boy, played by Craig Warnock, in the 1981 comedy "Time Bandits"?

4. Which city did the "Ghostbusters" save in 1984?

5. Who played the only lawyer willing to take Tom Hanks' case in "Philadelphia" in 1993?

6. Which 1977 comedy featured Burt Reynolds, Sally Field and a truckload of beer?

7. Who played the lead female role in the multi-Oscar winning 1985 film "Out of Africa"?

8. What was the name of the beauty in "Beauty and the Beast"?

9. Who were "protecting the Earth from the scum of the universe" in 1997?

10. True or False – the final chase scene in Hitchcock's "North by Northwest" was actually shot at Mount Rushmore.

ANSWERS:

1. Sam Neill

2. "Look Who's Talking"

3. Kevin

4. New York

5. Denzel Washington

6. "Smokey and the Bandit"

7. Meryl Streep

8. Belle

9. "Men In Black"

10. False (shot in studio as they could not get permission to film at Mt. Rushmore)

TAKE A CHANCE 31

In this round each correct answer is worth 2 points making a possible score of 20. However if you get any question wrong your score for this round is halved. If you are not sure, leave an answer blank and you still score 2 points for each correct answer (unless you get one wrong!)

1. Which athlete carried the flag for Great Britain at the closing ceremony of the 2004 Athens Olympic Games?

2. Who won an Oscar for directing the film "Dances with Wolves"?

3. Which cartoon character has an adopted son called Swee'pea?

4. Who was Marilyn Monroe's last husband?

5. What is the largest instrument in a concert orchestra?

6. Which construction in Australia begins at Dawes Point and ends at Milsons Point?

7. In which stories by Enid Blyton are siblings Julian, Dick and Anne sent to stay with their Aunt Fanny and Uncle Quentin?

8. Which musical instrument does Jim play in the BBC comedy "The Royle Family"?

9. Which is the only group to have a No 1 single containing the word Monday in its title?

10. In which European capital city was the Bloody Mary cocktail invented?

ANSWERS:

1. Kelly Holmes

2. Kevin Costner

3. Popeye

4. Arthur Miller

5. Piano

6. Sydney Harbour Bridge

7. "Famous Five"

8. Banjo

9. Boomtown Rats

10. Paris

POT LUCK 32

1. Dry ice is a solid form of which gas?

2. In which English county are the towns of Bodmin and Truro?

3. In which 1984 film did Daryl Hannah play a mermaid named Madison?

4. A 'Bridge of Sighs' can be found in Oxford and which other British city?

5. Who was US President between 1981 and 1989?

6. The hanger, rapier and cutlass are all types of what weapon?

7. After the collapse of Communism, who in 1991 was Russia's first democratically elected President?

8. The first US Space Shuttle was named after which fictional starship from the TV series "Star Trek"?

9. What is the common name for the condition dyspepsia?

10. Which vitamin is also known as retinol?

ANSWERS:

1. Carbon Dioxide

2. Cornwall

3. "Splash"

4. Cambridge

5. Ronald Reagan

6. Sword

7. Boris Yeltsin

8. Enterprise (Never Flew in Space)

9. Indigestion

10. Vitamin A

SONGS

1. Which song was a top 10 hit for Dusty Springfield, the Bay City rollers and the Tourists?

2. Which hit single features the line, "Now if I appear to be carefree, it's only to camouflage my sadness"?

3. What was the title of Take That's 2006 No 1 single, their first for over 10 years?

4. Which Oasis song features the line, "So I start a revolution from my bed"?

5. Which Wham! Song was a No. 1 hit in Britain and the USA?

6. Which 1982 No. 1 single was based on the Zulu folk tune "Wimoweh"?

7. Which 1979 No. 1 tells the story of San Diego schoolgirl Brenda Spencer?

8. "I saw the light on the night that I passed by her window", is a line from which song?

9. What was the first Spice Girls single not to reach No. 1 in the British charts?

10. Which Whitney Houston hit began a run of 10 weeks at No.1 in December 1992?

ANSWERS:

1. "I Only Want to be With You"
2. "Tears of a Clown"
3. "Patience"
4. "Don't Look Back in Anger"
5. "Wake Me Up Before You Go-Go"
6. "The Lion Sleeps Tonight"
7. "I Don't Like Mondays"
8. "Delilah"
9. "Stop"
10. "I Will Always Love You"

HOLIDAYS

1. Which singer had her first Top 10 hit in the UK charts in 1984 with "Holiday"?

2. In which country is the tourist area the Costa del Sol?

3. Which tourist resort is famous for 'The Golden Mile'?

4. Who was the singer with The Tourists?

5. What was the name of the holiday camp in Hi-De-Hi"?

6. Which pop singer starred in the film "Summer Holiday"?

7. Three friends spent their vacation on a cattle drive in which 1991 film?

8. Which seaside resort in New Jersey is known for its 'Boardwalk'?

9. Which pop group topped the charts in 1978 with "Dreadlock Holiday"?

10. Butlin's opened their first holiday camp in which resort?

ANSWERS:

1. Madonna

2. Spain

3. Blackpool

4. Annie Lennox

5. Maplins

6. Cliff Richard

7. "City Slickers"

8. Atlantic City

9. 10cc

10. Skegness

THIS IS MURDER

1. Who became Archbishop of Canterbury in 1162, eight years before his murder?

2. Which murderer is the subject of Norman Mailer's novel "The Executioner's Song"?

3. In which country was Joy Adamson murdered?

4. Who was hanged in 1953 for a murder carried out by 16 year old Christopher Craig?

5. Which of the Sex Pistols was arrested for the murder of Nancy Spungen in 1978?

6. Which Roman Emperor was murdered by his own guards in AD 41?

7. Who was the Egyptian President assassinated by rebel soldiers in 1981?

8. Which legendary music producer was first tried for the murder of actress Lana Clarkson in 2007?

9. Who murdered five London prostitutes in knife attacks in 1888?

10. Who was murdered by Mark Chapman in December 1980?

ANSWERS:

1. Thomas A'Becket

2. Gary Gilmore

3. Kenya

4. Derek Bentley

5. Sid Vicious

6. Caligula

7. Anwar Sadat

8. Phil Spector

9. Jack the Ripper

10. John Lennon

TAKE A CHANCE 32

In this round each correct answer is worth 2 points making a possible score of 20. However if you get any question wrong your score for this round is halved. If you are not sure, leave an answer blank and you still score 2 points for each correct answer (unless you get one wrong!)

1. Which actress starred in 9 "Carry On" films starting with "Carry on Spying" and ending with "Carry on Dick"?

2. What title is given to the longest serving MP in the House of Commons?

3. Who is the mother of Sean Lennon

4. Who was the first ever Briton in space?

5. Which famous singer was born above a fish & chip shop owned by her grandmother in Rochdale?

6. Which actor played the title role in the TV series "Raffles"?

7. Which English explorer was sponsored by Queen Elizabeth 1 for an expedition to the Pacific?

8. Which of these is actress Leslie Ash's real name – Lillian Ashworth, Janet Jones or Leslie Ash?

9. Which footballer has the distinction of being England's youngest and oldest goalkeeper?

10. Which female singer duetted with Bobby Brown on the 1994 hit "Something in Common"?

ANSWERS:

1. Barbara Windsor

2. Father of the House

3. Yoko Ono

4. Helen Sharman

5. Gracie Fields

6. Anthony Valentine

7. Sir Francis Drake

8. Leslie Ash

9. Peter Shilton

10. Whitney Houston

SEPTEMBER

POT LUCK 33

1. In the 1986 film 'Crocodile Dundee' what was the title character's first name?

2. The Chinook is a warm, dry wind that blows in which mountains?

3. In which county is the resort of Lyme Regis?

4. 'Entente Cordiale', refers to an understanding between Britain and which other European country?

5. Who, in Greek mythology, was the twin brother of Pollux?

6. Which city is the capital of Belgium?

7. What system for identifying crime suspects from features described by witnesses, was first used by police in 1959?

8. How many prongs does a tuning fork have?

9. What name is given to an American ten cent piece?

10. The film 'The Longest Day' deals with which event of World War II in June 1944?

ANSWERS:

1. Michael or Mick

2. Rockies

3. Dorset

4. France

5. Castor

6. Brussels

7. Identikit

8. 2

9. Dime

10. D-Day Landings

NEWSPAPERS

1. The newspaper called the Weatherfield Recorder is featured in which TV series?

2. The cartoon strip "The Gambols" is featured in which daily newspaper?

3. In the In the 1999 film "Runaway Bride" Richard Gere plays a reporter for which newspaper – New York Times, USA Today or Washington Post?

4. Which national daily newspaper was launched by Eddie Shah in 1986?

5. Which paper printed the headline "World War II Bomber Found On Moon"?

6. Which Evelyn Waugh comedy novel features journalist William Boot working for the Daily Beast?

7. Which famous newspaper is mentioned in the lyrics of the Bee Gee's hit "Stayin' Alive"?

8. In July 1987 Jeffrey Archer won a libel case against which daily newspaper and was subsequently convicted for perjury?

9. Which newspaper was the original sponsor of "Who Wants To Be A Millionaire"?

10. Which British Sunday newspaper has the largest circulation?

ANSWERS:

1. "Coronation Street"
2. Daily Express
3. USA Today
4. Today
5. Sunday Sport
6. "Scoop"
7. New York Times
8. Daily Star
9. The Sun
10. News of the World

TWINS

1. Which East End gangster twins loved their mother?

2. Where did Alice encounter Tweedledee and Tweedledum?

3. Ross & Norris McWhirter co-founded which best-selling book?

4. Which sport is played by the Minnesota Twins?

5. Jacob and Esau are the only twins to appear in which book?

6. How are Transylvanian twins Monica and Gabriela Irimia better known?

7. According to Roman legend, did Romulus kill Remus or did Remus kill Romulus?

8. For which country did Frank and Ronald de Boer play international football?

9. Who played the title roles in the 1988 film "Twins"? (One point for each)

10. Which 2007 TV programme featured twins Sam & Amanda Marchant?

ANSWERS:

1. Ronnie & Reggie Kray

2. "Through the Looking Glass"

3. "Guinness Book of Records"

4. Baseball

5. Bible

6. The Cheeky Girls

7. Romulus killed Remus

8. Netherlands

9. Danny DeVito & Arnold Schwarzenegger

10. "Big Brother 8"

TV SCI-FI COMEDY

1. Who played Gary Sparrow in "Goodnight, Sweetheart"?

2. The US TV series "Mork & Mindy" was a spin-off from which show?

3. Who was the alter ego of George Sunday in "My Hero"?

4. In the US TV series "ALF", what did ALF stand for?

5. Who played an Indian Dalek coming home from work in a sketch in the 70's series "Q6"?

6. In which series did a character say, "I am Holly, the ship's computer with an IQ of 6000. The same IQ as 6000 PE teachers"?

7. In which 60's series did Uncle Martin become invisible when antennae came out of his head?

8. What was the name of the computer in "Hitch-Hiker's Guide to the Galaxy" that answered the question of "life, the universe and everything"?

9. What was the Emmy award winning series created Matt Groening that followed "The Simpsons"?

10. In which US series did William Shatner make guest appearances as The Big Giant Head/Supreme Ruler of the Galaxy?

ANSWERS:

1. Nicholas Lyndhurst

2. "Happy Days"

3. Thermoman

4. Alien Life Form

5. Spike Milligan

6. "Red Dwarf"

7. "My Favourite Martian"

8. Deep Thought

9. "Futurama"

10. "3rd Rock from the Sun"

TAKE A CHANCE 33

In this round each correct answer is worth 2 points making a possible score of 20. However if you get any question wrong your score for this round is halved. If you are not sure, leave an answer blank and you still score 2 points for each correct answer (unless you get one wrong!)

1. Who succeeded Sue Lawley as the presenter of "Desert Island Discs"?

2. On which TV game show did Loyd Grossman frequently say, "Let's look at the evidence"?

3. At which event did the ants dance with the fleas?

4. Who was Prime Minister when the IRA fired three mortar shells at Downing Street in February 1991?

5. Which football legend once said, "I used to go missing a lot…Miss Canada, Miss United Kingdom, Miss World…"?

6. Oak Apple Day celebrated the restoration of which monarch to the throne?

7. In which Alfred Hitchcock thriller was James Stewart confined to a wheelchair?

8. Who is England's second most capped goalkeeper?

9. Which flag was first flown at Fort Stanwix in New York on 3rd August 1777?

10. Which 1974 No 1 hit told of Billy Chin and Sammy Chung?

ANSWERS:

1. Kirsty Young

2. "Through the Keyhole"

3. Ugly Bug Ball

4. John Major

5. George Best

6. Charles II

7. "Rear Window"

8. David Seaman

9. Stars & Stripes (US Flag)

10. "Kung Fu Fighting" (Carl Douglas)

POT LUCK 34

1. In which sport are the terms full toss, yorker and beamer used?

2. Pomme is the French word for which fruit?

3. Who was the last Anglo-Saxon King before the Norman Conquest?

4. Which coin was worth a quarter of an old English penny, and was taken from circulation in 1961?

5. In Italy, ricotta, pecorino and mascarpone are types of what?

6. What is a female fox called?

7. What number on the Beaufort scale is a wind described as a gale?

8. In which country was feminist writer Germaine Greer born?

9. The River Tamar flows along the border of Devon and which other county?

10. In Greek legend, Jason and the Argonauts went in search of what?

ANSWERS:

1. Cricket

2. Apple

3. Harold

4. Farthing

5. Cheese

6. Vixen

7. 8

8. Australia

9. Cornwall

10. Golden Fleece

TRANSPORTATION

1. According to Chinese philosopher Lao Tzu, "A journey of 1000 miles begins with…" what?

2. Name the Brunel steamship, launched in 1843, that was removed from the Falklands to be restored in Bristol?

3. Which company operates passenger train services throughout the USA?

4. Which company produced the first commercial jet airliner?

5. The name of which 19th Century industrialist has become synonymous with luxury railway cars?

6. What starts at Gas Street Basin and ends at Diglis Basin?

7. If you were going somewhere on 'Shanks's pony", how would you be travelling?

8. Which new London Underground line was built between 1968 and 1971?

9. What is usually transported on a Ro-Ro ship?

10. What will be the name of Virgin Galactic's first tourist space ship?

ANSWERS:

1. "A single step"

2. SS Great Britain

3. Amtrak

4. De Havilland (Comet)

5. George Pullman

6. Worcester & Birmingham Canal

7. Walking/On Foot

8. Victoria

9. Vehicles (Roll On – Roll Off Ferry)

10. VSS Enterprise

MONEY, MONEY, MONEY

1. Which group had a Top 3 hit in 1976 with "Money, Money, Money"?

2. In finance, what does APR stand for?

3. Who wrote the novel "Hot Money" which features jockey Ian Pembroke as the main character?

4. The Bundesbank is the state bank of which country?

5. "The Colour of Money" was the sequel to which film?

6. Which institution is responsible for issuing bank notes in England and Wales?

7. What is the term for a speculator who buys shares on the Stock Exchange in anticipation of rising prices to make a profit when selling?

8. Which American film director said in 1976, "Money is better than poverty, if only for financial reasons"?

9. Before the Euro, what was the currency of Holland?

10. In "Monopoly", how much money do you collect when you pass "Go"?

ANSWERS:

1. Abba

2. Annual Percentage Rate

3. Dick Francis

4. Germany

5. "The Hustler"

6. Bank of England

7. Bull

8. Woody Allen

9. Guilder (or Florin)

10. £200

EAT, DRINK & BE MERRY

1. Complete this advertising slogan, "Don't say brown, say...."

2. What fruit juice is used in a Harvey Wallbanger?

3. What canned soup, introduced in 1897, was immortalised by American artist Andy Warhol?

4. Which herb is used in pesto sauce providing its green colour?

5. The image of what animal is stamped on eggs as a mark of quality?

6. What was advertised in the '90's with the slogan "Not everything in black & white makes sense"?

7. Which country produces almost 75% of the world's coffee?

8. Which musical instrument is known as a "liquorice stick" in Jazz circles?

9. Which 20ᵗʰ century British Prime Minister had Pol Roger champagne specially bottled in Imperial one pint bottles?

10. In which country did Conference Pears originate?

ANSWERS:

1. Hovis

2. Orange Juice

3. Campbell's

4. Basil

5. Lion

6. Guinness

7. Brazil (33.2% in 2006)

8. Clarinet

9. Winston Churchill

10. Britain

TAKE A CHANCE 34

In this round each correct answer is worth 2 points making a possible score of 20. However if you get any question wrong your score for this round is halved. If you are not sure, leave an answer blank and you still score 2 points for each correct answer (unless you get one wrong!)

1. In which TV show did one of the central characters often say, "I love it when a plan comes together"?

2. Into which bay does the River Ganges flow?

3. "He was only ten years old when his daddy died in prison" was a line from which Kenny Rogers hit?

4. Who famously said, "A woman rang to say she heard there was a hurricane on the way. Well, don't worry there isn't"?

5. The Gasworks Gang are the enemy of which character in the "Beano"?

6. Which hell raising British actor once stripped naked in a Madrid restaurant and dived into an aquarium?

7. Which manager walked out on the England team in 1977 to take a lucrative job in Dubai?

8. As PC184, which snooker player received a commendation for disarming a man with a shotgun?

9. What was the call sign of Kris Kristofferson's character in the film "Convoy"?

10. Which TV presenter once asked the family group the Corrs how they met – Jayne Middlemiss, Kelly Brook or Donna Air?

ANSWERS:

1. "The A-Team"
2. Bay of Bengal
3. "Coward of the County"
4. Michael Fish
5. Lord Snooty
6. Oliver Reed
7. Don Revie
8. Ray Reardon
9. Rubber Duck
10. Donna Air

POT LUCK 35

1. Which biblical character was sold into slavery by his jealous brothers?

2. Which film hero is known as 'Mr Kiss Kiss Bang Bang' in Italy?

3. On each Apollo moon landing, how many astronauts walked on the surface of the moon?

4. Which Electric Light Orchestra hit was featured on Atomic Kitten's single "Be With You"?

5. Which motorway encircles Manchester?

6. Which rock 'n' Roll legend was appointed a Special Agent of the Bureau of Narcotics & Dangerous Drugs?

7. A pugilist takes part in which sport?

8. What was the name of Jim Hawkins' ship in "Treasure Island"?

9. Which famous Disney film features the characters King Louie, Bagheera, Baloo and Shere Khan?

10. In which 1970's sitcom did one of the central characters give up his job in an attempt to become self-sufficient?

ANSWERS:

1. Joseph

2. James Bond

3. 2

4. "Last Train to London"

5. M60

6. Elvis Presley

7. Boxing

8. Hispaniola

9. "The Jungle Book"

10. "The Good Life"

DOUBLE ENGLISH

1. Which South American member of the camel family spits profusely when annoyed?

2. What was the title of Britney spear's 3rd UK chart topper, reaching No. 1 in May 2000?

3. Name the market town in Clwyd where the International Eisteddfod is held each year.

4. Who was Moses elder brother and co-leader of the Hebrews in their exodus from Egypt?

5. What is the more common name for the insecticide Dichloro-diphenyltrichloroethane?

6. Whose register of shipping, founded in 1760, provides rules for construction and maintenance?

7. What is the common name for any fish of the order Anguilliformes?

8. What is the name of the world's oldest independent railway company that still runs steam trains between Blaenau and Porthmadog?

9. Which American singer, killed in a plane crash, had a posthumous UK No 1 in January 2002?

10. Who created Winnie the Pooh?

ANSWERS:

1. Llama
2. "Oops…I Did it Again"
3. Llangollen
4. Aaron
5. DDT
6. Lloyd's (Register of Shipping)
7. Eel
8. Ffestiniog Railway
9. Aaliyah
10. A A Milne

SCHOOL DAYS

1. Which singer topped the UK singles chart with "School's Out" in 1972?

2. In which town is Charterhouse public school?

3. "Play School" was the first programme broadcast on which TV channel?

4. Which fictional girl's school was created by Ronald Searle?

5. Which 20th Century English artist painted "Coming Out of School"?

6. In which TV series did John Alderton play teacher Bernard Hedges?

7. "Tom Brown's Schooldays" is set at which school?

8. Whose chart topping 2001 album was entitled "Just Enough Education To Perform"?

9. Who played the headmaster of Hope Park Comprehensive School in the BBC series "Hope & Glory"?

10. Which 1980 film was set at the New York City School for the Performing Arts?

ANSWERS:

1. Alice Cooper

2. Godalming

3. BBC 2

4. St Trinian's

5. L S Lowry

6. "Please Sir"

7. Rugby

8. Stereophonics

9. Lenny Henry

10. "Fame"

FILM STARS

1. Which actor was arrested in 1995 after a liaison with prostitute Divine Brown?

2. Who directed the 1990 film "Dick Tracy"?

3. Which actress is associated with the line, "I want to be alone"?

4. Which actor starred in the 2000 film "The Green Mile"?

5. Who won a Best Supporting Actress Oscar for her performance as Velma Kelly in "Chicago"?

6. By what name is Lady Haden-Guest better known?

7. The real name of which actor, singer and comedian was Dino Paul Crocetti?

8. Which actor starred in the film "Kramer Vs. Kramer"?

9. Which film actor was Mr Universe in 1969?

10. Which actor played Indiana Jones in the movies?

ANSWERS:

1. Hugh Grant

2. Warren Beatty

3. Greta Garbo

4. Tom Hanks

5. Robin Williams

6. Jamie Lee Curtis

7. Dean Martin

8. Dustin Hoffman

9. Arnold Schwarzenegger

10. Harrison Ford

TAKE A CHANCE 35

In this round each correct answer is worth 2 points making a possible score of 20. However if you get any question wrong your score for this round is halved. If you are not sure, leave an answer blank and you still score 2 points for each correct answer (unless you get one wrong!)

1. Which is the only bird that walks upright?

2. The Righteous Brothers hit "Unchained Melody" reached No 1 in 1990 after being used in which film?

3. Which European capital city is mentioned in the lyrics of Men at Work's No 1 hit "Down Under"?

4. What was the name of the kebab shop owner played by Harry Enfield?

5. In which city is the Nobel Institute?

6. What was the name of the wife of Roger Rabbit?

7. Which radio station returned to the airwaves in August 1983, three years after the previous ship it broadcast from had sunk?

8. Which TV lawyer lived in the fictional town of San Remo in a camper van?

9. On which island is former Labour leader John Smith buried?

10. Which Englishman has scored 10 goals in World Cup tournaments?

ANSWERS:

1. Penguin
2. "Ghost"
3. Brussels
4. Stavros
5. Stockholm
6. Jessica
7. Radio Caroline
8. Petrocelli
9. Iona
10. Gary Lineker

POT LUCK 36

1. What was the name of the hippo in the children's TV series 'Rainbow?

2. Lieutenant Pinkerton and Cho Cho San are characters in which Puccini opera?

3. Barbershop' is a style of close harmony singing that traditionally incorporates how many male voices?

4. Which Lincolnshire town on the River Witham is the birthplace of Margaret Thatcher?

5. Singer Bryan Adams was born in which country?

6. What was the name of Ellen MacArthur's boat that she sailed around the world in the Vendee Globe 2000/2001 race?

7. Who had a number one UK album in 2000 with 'No Angel?

8. In the human body, what is produced by the lachrymal glands?

9. What name is given to the offspring of a male donkey and a female horse?

10. John Adams was the second holder of which office from 1797 until 1801?

ANSWERS:

1. George

2. "Madame Butterfly"

3. 4

4. Grantham

5. Canada

6. Kingfisher

7. Dido

8. Tears

9. Mule

10. US President

FUN FUN FUN

1. In which year did Disneyland Paris open (as Euro Disney)?

2. On which Blackpool rollercoaster did Richard Rodriguez spend 47 days in 1998?

3. Which group backed the Fun Boy Three on "It Ain't What You Do, It's The Way That You Do It"?

4. Which singer starred in the film "Fun In Acapulco"?

5. In which county is Thorpe Park?

6. Which singer topped the UK charts in July 2000 with "Life is a Rollercoaster"?

7. Who was the singer with the chart-topping group Fairground Attraction?

8. Which partnership composed the musical "Carousel"?

9. Which group topped the UK singles charts in 1995 with "Fairground"?

10. In which major American city is Disneyland?

ANSWERS:

1. 1992

2. The Big Dipper

3. Bananarama

4. Elvis Presley

5. Surrey

6. Ronan Keating

7. Eddi Reader

8. Rodgers & Hammerstein

9. Simply Red

10. Los Angeles (Anaheim)

EXTRA TIME

1. Who played Lionel in the TV sitcom "As Time Goes By"?

2. Which former Labour politician wrote his autobiography, "The Time of My Life", in 1989?

3. Which British playwright wrote the play "Old Times" in 1970?

4. Who devised and co-wrote the musical "Time"?

5. Which actress starred in the 1996 film "A Time to Kill"?

6. Which group topped the charts in 1989 with "Ride on Time"?

7. According to the proverb, a stitch in time saves…what?

8. The song "Time Warp" is featured in which musical?

9. Whose last words were, "I am just going outside and may be some time"?

10. Who wrote the novel "The Land That Time Forgot"?

ANSWERS:

1. Geoffrey Palmer

2. Denis Healey

3. Harold Pinter

4. Dave Clark

5. Sandra Bullock

6. Black Box

7. Nine

8. "The Rocky Horror Show"

9. Captain Lawrence Oates

10. Edgar Rice Burroughs

FILMS 03

1. Which actress starred in the films "Bull Durham" and "Lorenzo's Oil"?

2. The film "One Spy Too Many" was based on which 60's TV series?

3. Which 1996 film starred Bette Midler, Diane Keaton and Goldie Hawn?

4. In which series of films does Bruce Willis play a character called John McClane?

5. Which actor starred in the film "Disclosure"?

6. Who won his 2nd Oscar for his role in the 2007 film "There Will Be Blood"?

7. Which author is the subject of the film "Shadowlands"?

8. Which actor starred in the "Mission: Impossible" series of films?

9. In which 1959 did two musicians witness the St Valentine's Day Massacre?

10. What is the name of the character played by Heather Graham in "Austin Powers: The Spy Who Shagged Me"?

ANSWERS:

1. Susan Sarandon

2. "The Man From UNCLE"

3. "First Wives Club"

4. "Die Hard"

5. Michael Douglas

6. Daniel Day-Lewis

7. C S Lewis

8. Tom Cruise

9. "Some Like It Hot"

10. Felicity Shagwell

TAKE A CHANCE 36

In this round each correct answer is worth 2 points making a possible score of 20. However if you get any question wrong your score for this round is halved. If you are not sure, leave an answer blank and you still score 2 points for each correct answer (unless you get one wrong!)

1. In 2002, who removed her prosthetic leg during an interview with Larry King?

2. Which No 1 hit contains the lyric, "Life in plastic, it's fantastic"?

3. What breed of dog gave its name to a company making toy cars?

4. Russians referred to which Prime Minister as the 'British Bulldog'?

5. All but 3 minutes of which film starring Henry Fonda took place in a jury room?

6. Who accidentally shot his friend lawyer Harry Whittington in February 2006?

7. Which future French leader was wounded 3 times in WWI and captured by the Germans in 1916?

8. Andre Agassi won his first Grand Slam singles title at which event?

9. Which character in the Dandy is apparently the world's strongest man, able to lift a cow with one hand?

10. Which 1970's sitcom starred Jack Smethurst, Kate Williams, Rudolph Walker and Nina Baden-Semper?

ANSWERS:

1. Heather Mills McCartney
2. "Barbie Girl" by Aqua
3. Corgi
4. Sir Winston Churchill
5. "12 Angry Men"
6. Dick Cheney
7. Charles de Gaulle
8. Wimbledon (1992)
9. Desperate Dan
10. "Love Thy Neighbour"

POT LUCK 37

1. What are the little people called in the film 'The Wizard of Oz'?

2. What is the name of the piece of metal which hangs inside a bell?

3. The United States became involved in which major conflict in Asia in 1950?

4. In the TV comedy series 'Father Ted', what was the name of the housekeeper?

5. How many beats in a bar does a waltz usually have?

6. Which Yorkshire fishing port links Captain Cook and Count Dracula?

7. What is the name of Bob the Builder's cat?

8. What would be your sporting pastime if you used crampons and pitons?

9. The standard British one pound coin is made of an alloy of copper, nickel and which other metallic element?

10. What Christian name was shared by three of Henry VIII's wives?

ANSWERS:

1. Munchkins

2. Clapper

3. Korean War

4. Mrs Doyle

5. 3

6. Whitby

7. Pilchard

8. Mountaineering

9. Zinc

10. Catherine

OLD AND NEW

1. Which 1993 movie reunited Jack Lemmon and Walter Matthau?

2. What was the name of Prince's backing band on 10 UK chart hits from 1991 – 93?

3. What is the popular name for the Central Criminal Court in London?

4. Which 1932 novel features characters Bernard Marx and Mustapha Mond?

5. Ernest Hemingway won a Pulitzer Prize in 1953 for which novel?

6. Former "Emmerdale" actress Malandra Burrows was the youngest ever winner on which TV talent show?

7. Leonard Sachs was the chairman on which show?

8. Joe DiMaggio played baseball for which club?

9. What is the first property on a "Monopoly" board after Go?

10. What was the title of Stephen Gately's first solo UK hit single and album in 2000?

ANSWERS:

1. "Grumpy Old Men"

2. The New Power Generation

3. Old Bailey

4. "Brave New World

5. "The Old Man and the Sea"

6. "New Faces"

7. "The Good Old Days"

8. New York Yankees

9. Old Kent Road

10. "New Beginning"

MAGIC MOMENTS

1. Which singer had a No. 1 in 1958 with "Magic Moments"?

2. Who composed the opera "The Magic Flute"?

3. Which character, played by Bill Maynard, used the catchphrase, "Magic"?

4. What famous landmark was made to disappear in "The Magic of David Copperfield V" in 1983?

5. Which group had a Top 10 hit in 1992 with a version of Barry Manilow's "Could It Be Magic"?

6. Magic Johnson played for which basketball team?

7. What was the name of the snail in "The Magic Roundabout"?

8. Which sport is played by the Orlando Magic?

9. Which group had a UK No. 1 in 1981 with "Every Little Thing She Does Is Magic"?

10. In which 1956 film did Marilyn Monroe sing "That Old Black Magic"?

ANSWERS:

1. Perry Como

2. Mozart

3. Selwyn Froggitt

4. Statue of Liberty

5. Take That

6. Los Angeles Lakers

7. Brian

8. Basketball

9. Police

10. "Bus Stop"

GREAT BRITONS

1. Who directed the BAFTA Award winning 1993 film "Shadowlands"?

2. Who said, "England expects every man to do his duty"?

3. Who formulated the Laws of Gravity?

4. Which Scottish poet was born in Alloway in 1759?

5. Which Prime Minister introduced the 'Right to Buy' for council tenants?

6. Who captained Manchester United to victory in the 1968 European Cup Final?

7. Who composed "The Enigma Variations"?

8. Which actor starred in the film "Howard's End"?

9. Which Victorian engineer and his achievements were commemorated on two 2006 £2 coins?

10. Which famous singer was once a member of the Dick Teague Skiffle Group?

ANSWERS:

1. Richard Attenborough

2. Lord Nelson

3. Sir Isaac Newton

4. Robert Burns

5. Margaret Thatcher

6. Bobby Charlton

7. Edward Elgar

8. Anthony Hopkins

9. Isambard Kingdom Brunel

10. Cliff Richard

TAKE A CHANCE 37

In this round each correct answer is worth 2 points making a possible score of 20. However if you get any question wrong your score for this round is halved. If you are not sure, leave an answer blank and you still score 2 points for each correct answer (unless you get one wrong!)

1. Which of the world's capital cities is the first to celebrate New Year?

2. What colour are the seats in the House of Lords?

3. Which novel opens with the line, "Renowned curator Jacques Sauniere staggered through the vaulted archway of the museum's Grand Gallery"?

4. Who was nominated for a Best Supporting Actress Oscar for her role in "Steel Magnolias" as a young bride battling diabetes?

5. What is the name of the cow in the pantomime "Jack & the Beanstalk"?

6. Which fictional villain fell over the Reichenbach Falls after struggling with Sherlock Holmes?

7. Which club has played every season in the Premier League since it began and has never finished in the Top 4?

8. Which hit by the Specials featured the line, "Bands won't play no more, too much fighting on the dance floor"?

9. Which actress was eight months pregnant when she was murdered at her home in Benedict Canyon, Los Angeles in August 1969?

10. Patrick and Pippa Trench were the neighbours of the central characters in which sitcom?

ANSWERS:

1. Wellington
2. Red
3. "The Da Vinci Code"
4. Julia Roberts
5. Buttercup
6. Professor Moriarty
7. Tottenham Hotspur
8. "Ghost Town"
9. Sharon Tate
10. "One Foot in the Grave"

POT LUCK 38

1. The lyre-bird and the kookaburra are native to which country?

2. Which British city has postcodes that begin with BS?

3. Which Essex seaside resort has the world's longest pleasure pier?

4. Which lively dance of Bohemian origin shares its name with a pattern of bold dots usually on fabric?

5. Which vegetable is called aloo on Indian menus?

6. The American Plane 'Enola Gay' was the first to drop what type of weapon?

7. What is the nickname of Watford FC?

8. Where would an Inuit wear his mukluks?

9. In politics, which member of the Government is also Minister for the Civil Service?

10. What 'D' is the name of the currency in Jordan, Tunisia and Iraq?

ANSWERS:

1. Australia

2. Bristol

3. Southend-on-Sea

4. Polka

5. Potato

6. Atom Bomb

7. Hornets

8. On His Feet

9. Prime Minister

10. Dinar

FILMS 04

1. What was Ace Ventura's profession according to the title of the 1994 film?

2. Which series of films features the robots C3PO and R2-D2?

3. Danny Zuko is a leading character in which film musical?

4. Who starred as Batman in the 1997 film 'Batman and Robin'?

5. Which 'Madonna' hit was first heard in the 1985 film 'Desperately Seeking Susan'?

6. Which artist was portrayed by Kirk Douglas in the film 'Lust for Life'?

7. Who won the Best Actress Oscar for her portrayal of Ada in the 1993 film "The Piano"?

8. Who reprised his role as palaeontologist, Dr Alan Grant, in the film sequel, 'Jurassic Park III'?

9. In the 1939 film 'The Wizard of Oz', what did the Scarecrow ask the Wizard to give him?

10. Who plays Gandalf in the film, 'The Lord of the Rings: The Fellowship of the Ring'?

ANSWERS:

1. Pet Detective

2. "Star Wars"

3. "Grease"

4. George Clooney

5. "Into the Groove"

6. Vincent Van Gogh

7. Holly Hunter

8. Sam Neill

9. Brain

10. Sir Ian McKellen

FOOD & DRINK

1. The nouvelle cuisine style of cooking originated in which country?

2. The drink Perry is made from which fruit?

3. Which spirit takes its name from the Gaelic for "water of life"?

4. What is the main ingredient of Bombay Duck?

5. Feta cheese is made in which country?

6. The dish chop suey originated in which country?

7. Which cocktail is made from Champagne and orange juice?

8. In which month is Beaujolais Nouveau released for consumption?

9. The dish guacamole is from which country?

10. Which drink was invented by Dr John Pemberton in 1886?

ANSWERS:

1. France

2. Pears

3. Whisky

4. Fish

5. Greece

6. United States of America

7. Bucks Fizz

8. November

9. Mexico

10. Coca Cola

LETTERS

1. Scurvy is an illness caused by a deficiency of which vitamin?

2. What is next in the sequence: Q, W, E, R, T, Y?

3. Which character was played by John Cleese in the 2002 Bond film "Die Another Day"?

4. Which Roman numeral represents the number 5?

5. What is the chemical symbol for potassium?

6. Which letter in Morse Code is represented by a single dot?

7. What was US President Harry Truman's middle initial?

8. What is the most common blood group in the world?

9. What is the international identification letter for cars from Germany?

10. Robin Scott had a No. 2 hit in 1979 with "Pop Muzik" under what name?

ANSWERS:

1. C

2. U (I, O, P)

3. Q

4. V

5. K

6. E

7. S

8. O

9. D

10. M

TAKE A CHANCE 38

In this round each correct answer is worth 2 points making a possible score of 20. However if you get any question wrong your score for this round is halved. If you are not sure, leave an answer blank and you still score 2 points for each correct answer (unless you get one wrong!)

1. What is the largest, oldest and most well known high IQ society in the world?

2. Which famous film director and producer died of lung cancer on 15th December 1966 at the age of 65?

3. Who defeated 134 other candidates to win the election to become Governor of California in 2003?

4. Cartoon mice Pixie and Dixie frequently out-witted which cat?

5. In which sitcom is Dr Piers Crispin "Britain's favourite TV doctor"?

6. "If You Tolerate this Your Children Will Be Next" gave which band their first UK No 1 single?

7. Which former Formula 1 World Champion was nicknamed 'The Flying Scot'?

8. Which Radio 2 DJ is often referred to as 'The Togmeister'?

9. Starring Tom Cruise and Max von Sydow, which film is set in Washington DC during the year 2054?

10. Darren Lamb and Maggie Jacobs are central characters in which TV comedy show?

ANSWERS:

1. MENSA International
2. Walt Disney
3. Arnold Schwarzenegger
4. Mr Jinks
5. "My Hero"
6. Manic Street Preachers
7. Jackie Stewart
8. Terry Wogan
9. "Minority Report"
10. "Extras"

POT LUCK 39

1. Who won his second Best Actor Oscar for the title role in the film 'Forrest Gump?

2. Michael Bloomberg succeeded Rudy Giuliani as Mayor of which American city in 2002?

3. Which British crime novelist wrote 'Murder at the Vicarage' and 'Murder in Mesopotamia'?

4. In which English county is the city of Portsmouth?

5. Which Premier League football club's home ground is the Reebok Stadium?

6. Which colour does Philadelphia-born singer, Alicia Moore, use as her stage name?

7. What word means to distribute playing cards among players?

8. What name was given to buried treasure, which became the property of the Crown?

9. Which tunnel under the Thames was the world's longest when it opened in 1897?

10. Which British Duke led allied forces in the decisive victory over Napoleon at Waterloo?

ANSWERS:

1. Tom Hanks

2. New York

3. Agatha Christie

4. Hampshire

5. Bolton Wanderers

6. Pink

7. Deal

8. Treasure Trove

9. Blackwall

10. Wellington

BLACK & WHITE

1. Which country music singer was nicknamed 'The Man in Black'?

2. Which sport is played by the Chicago White Sox?

3. What type of creature is a black widow?

4. Which singer had a Top 10 hit in the 1980's with "White Wedding"?

5. In which country is the Black Forest?

6. Which British artist painted "The White Horse" in 1819?

7. Which group had a No 1 in the 1960's with "Paint It Black"?

8. With which board game would you associate Mrs White?

9. Who wrote the TV series "The Boys from the Black Stuff"?

10. Which South African fast bowler was nicknamed 'White Lightning'?

ANSWERS:

1. Johnny Cash

2. Baseball

3. Spider

4. Billy Idol

5. Germany

6. John Constable

7. Rolling Stones

8. Cluedo

9. Alan Bleasdale

10. Allan Donald

INITIAL SUCCESS 05

The first letter of each answer to questions 1 – 9 spells out the name of a sporting venue. Question 10 relates to that sporting venue.

1. The song "America" is featured in which musical?

2. Which pop duo was formed by Andy Bell and Vince Clarke?

3. Which actress and model 'married' Dale Winton in a spoof TV documentary about his life?

4. What was Michael Jackson's first solo No 1 album in the UK charts?

5. What colour is the cross on the Scottish flag?

6. Which 1960's Oscar winning film featured Oliver Reed as Bill Sikes?

7. What is Europe's most northerly capital city?

8. After shooting a villain with a spear gun, in which film did James Bond say, "I think he got the point"?

9. Who won an Oscar for Best Actress in the 2004 film "Million Dollar Baby"?

10. This is a famous venue for which sport?

ANSWERS:

1. "West Side Story"

2. Erasure

3. Nell McAndrew

4. "Thriller"

5. White

6. "Oliver!"

7. Reykjavík

8. "Thunderball"

9. Hilary Swank

10. Golf

AMERICAN TV

1. Which actor played Dan in the TV series "Roseanne"?

2. Which TV series featured Mr Chekov and Mr Sulu?

3. In which city was "Frasier" set?

4. What was the name of the central character in "The Fugitive"?

5. Which actress played the title role in the TV series "Dr Quinn: Medicine Woman"?

6. Which character in "Cheers" hailed from Hanover, Indiana?

7. Which series follows the survivors of the crashed Oceanic Flight 815 from Sydney to Los Angeles?

8. Which musical instrument is played by Lisa Simpson?

9. Which actor played Ross & Monica's father Jack in "Friends"?

10. "Knots Landing" was a spin off from which long running soap opera?

ANSWERS:

1. John Goodman

2. "Star Trek"

3. Seattle

4. Dr Richard Kimble

5. Jane Seymour

6. Woody Boyd

7. "Lost"

8. Saxophone

9. Elliott Gould

10. "Dallas"

TAKE A CHANCE 39

In this round each correct answer is worth 2 points making a possible score of 20. However if you get any question wrong your score for this round is halved. If you are not sure, leave an answer blank and you still score 2 points for each correct answer (unless you get one wrong!)

1. Second Division Sunderland defeated which club in the 1973 FA Cup Final?

2. Which golf course is known as 'The Home of Golf'?

3. Which character in "It Ain't Half Hot Mum" frequently said, "Shoulders back, lovely boy"?

4. Which former model is perhaps the most famous ambassador of the Adopt-a-Minefield charity?

5. In which decade was Diet Pepsi first launched in the USA?

6. Which actress played Ruth Ellis in the 1985 film "Dance with a Stranger"?

7. Which famous musical tells of a chorus girl called Christine, the daughter of a prominent violinist?

8. Which Conservative MP unsuccessfully challenged John Major for the leadership of the party in 1995?

9. Jimmy Olsen is a reporter and Perry White is the Chief Editor for which fictional newspaper?

10. Who is pictured smoking a marijuana joint on the cover of the 1973 album "Catch a Fire"?

ANSWERS:

1. Leeds United
2. St Andrews
3. Sgt-Major Williams
4. Heather Mills McCartney
5. 1960's (1964)
6. Miranda Richardson
7. "The Phantom of the Opera"
8. John Redwood
9. Daily Planet
10. Bob Marley

POT LUCK 40

1. In South African currency, one hundred cents make up one... what?

2. Robbie Williams and Nicole Kidman entered the charts at number one in December 2001 with a cover of which song?

3. 'Toad of Toad Hall' is a dramatic adaptation of which Kenneth Grahame children's book?

4. In which decade did the Spanish Civil War take place?

5. Which famous ballet company was founded in Moscow in 1776?

6. Which painter immortalised the dancer Jane Avril in his posters for the Moulin Rouge?

7. The Transporter Bridge in Middlesbrough spans which river?

8. How many different portraits of the Queen have been used on British coins?

9. Which city has the only natural hot springs in Great Britain?

10. What did the 'J' stand for in the initials of the fantasy writer J. R. R. Tolkien?

ANSWERS:

1. Rand

2. "Somethin' Stupid"

3. "The Wind in the Willows"

4. 1930's

5. Bolshoi

6. Toulouse-Lautrec

7. Tees

8. 4

9. Bath

10. John

HALLOWEEN

1. Which actress won an Oscar playing a psychic in the 1990 film "Ghost"?

2. What is the term for a male witch?

3. Which Shakespearean character is haunted by the ghost of Banquo?

4. Who wrote "The Lion, The Witch and the Wardrobe"?

5. In which city is "Ghostbusters" set?

6. Twenty people were executed after witchcraft trial in which Massachusetts town in 1692?

7. Which company manufactures the Silver Ghost motor car?

8. What is the name of the sea witch in "The Little Mermaid"?

9. Which pop group had a No 1 hit with "Ghost Town" in 1981?

10. Which 1999 film follows three student filmmakers who disappear in the woods?

ANSWERS:

1. Whoopi Goldberg

2. Warlock

3. Macbeth

4. C S Lewis

5. New York

6. Salem

7. Rolls Royce

8. Ursula

9. Specials

10. "The Blair Witch Project"

20TH CENTURY

1. Which town in the Ukraine was the site of a major nuclear disaster in 1986?

2. In which year did the Second World War end?

3. Which rock 'n' roll singer died in a plane crash along with the Big Bopper and Richie Valens?

4. What was the name of the German airship that exploded in New Jersey in May 1937?

5. Who was President of the United States at the outbreak of WWI?

6. Who married Commander Tim Lawrence in December 1992?

7. Who was Prime Minister at the time of the General Strike in 1926?

8. Who was the leader of the Suffragettes that founded the Women's Social & Political Union in 1903?

9. Olaf Palme was the Prime Minister of which country when he was assassinated in 1986?

10. The Soviet Union invaded which country in 1979?

ANSWERS:

1. Chernobyl

2. 1945

3. Buddy Holly

4. Hindenburg

5. Woodrow Wilson

6. Princess Anne

7. Stanley Baldwin

8. Emmeline Pankhurst

9. Sweden

10. Afghanistan

SPORT

1. Which British athlete was disqualified from the Men's 100 metres final at the 1996 Olympics?

2. Which boxer did Muhammad Ali fight in 'The Thriller in Manila'?

3. Which jockey rode all 7 winners at Ascot in September 1996?

4. Which London football club play their home games at the Boleyn Ground? (known by another name)

5. Who won the World Snooker title in 1972 and 1982?

6. Which tennis player won her seventh Wimbledon Ladies' Singles title in 1996?

7. Bryan Habana plays Rugby Union for which country?

8. Which motor racing circuit is the venue for the Italian Grand Prix?

9. Which Australian golfer won the British Open in 1986 and 1993?

10. Which England batsman passed Geoff Boycott's record of test runs in 1992?

ANSWERS:

1. Linford Christie

2. Joe Frazier

3. Frankie Dettori

4. West Ham United

5. Alex Higgins

6. Steffi Graf

7. South Africa

8. Monza

9. Greg Norman

10. David Gower

TAKE A CHANCE 40

In this round each correct answer is worth 2 points making a possible score of 20. However if you get any question wrong your score for this round is halved. If you are not sure, leave an answer blank and you still score 2 points for each correct answer (unless you get one wrong!)

1. Who was the best man at Hugh Laurie's wedding and is godfather to his 3 children?

2. Karachi is a major seaport in which country?

3. Situated in Bloomsbury in London, what is generally regarded as the most prestigious drama school in the world?

4. Which chart topper by the Police features the line, "Strong words in the staff room; the accusations fly"?

5. Which British comedian and actor describes himself as an "executive transvestite"?

6. Which Austrian driver won the 1984 Formula 1 World Championship by half a point?

7. Who served as Prime Minister on 4 occasions and also holds the record for the longest continuous service as an MP at over 62 years?

8. Herb Powell is the half brother of which fictional character?

9. Which former tennis star makes an appearance as himself in the 2003 film "Anger Management"?

10. Who was the first cartoon character to be depicted on a US postage stamp?

ANSWERS:

1. Stephen Fry
2. Pakistan
3. RADA (Royal Academy of Dramatic Art)
4. "Don't Stand So Close To Me"
5. Eddie Izzard
6. Niki Lauda
7. William Gladstone
8. Homer Simpson
9. John McEnroe
10. Bugs Bunny (1997)

NOVEMBER

POT LUCK 41

1. What was the name of the Chinese dynasty that reigned from 1368 to 1644?

2. What name is given to the last man of a Tug of War team or the runner of the last leg in a relay race?

3. What was the name given to the Dutch settlers in South Africa?

4. In 1981, Francois Mitterrand became President of which country?

5. In which English county would you find Stoke-on-Trent?

6. Which British city would you associate with the comedians Ken Dodd and Jimmy Tarbuck?

7. Who was the first vocalist to front the 1970's heavy rock band 'Black Sabbath'?

8. In which pastime would you use 'Flies', 'Plugs', 'Spinners' and 'Spoons'?

9. Tchaikovsky's 1812 Overture commemorates Napoleon's retreat from which city?

10. In which century was the American War of Independence?

ANSWERS:

1. Ming

2. Anchorman

3. Boers

4. France

5. Staffordshire

6. Liverpool

7. Ozzy Osbourne

8. Angling

9. Moscow

10. 18th (1700's)

KEEPING UP WITH THE JONESES

1. What title does Sophie Rhys-Jones possess since her marriage to Prince Edward?

2. Which actress starred in the Bridget Jones movies?

3. Gloria Jones survived the car crash that killed which singer in 1977?

4. Vinnie Jones played football for which country?

5. The musical "Carmen Jones" is based on whose opera?

6. Which actress starred in the 70's sitcom "Miss Jones & Son" and more recently played Lillian in the cult comedy "The Smoking Room"?

7. Which group joined Tom Jones on the 1999 hit "Burning Down the House"?

8. Who directed the "Indiana Jones" films?

9. Which actor played Corporal Jones in "Dad's Army"?

10. Which Scandinavian group had a UK No 1 in 1998 with "Doctor Jones"?

ANSWERS:

1. Countess Wessex

2. Renée Zellweger

3. Marc Bolan

4. Wales

5. Bizet

6. Paula Wilcox

7. Cardigans

8. Stephen Spielberg

9. Clive Dunn

10. Aqua

SAINTS ALIVE (All Saints Day)

1. Which Russian city was previously called Petrograd?
2. Who was the first Pope?
3. Which 80's hospital drama starred Ed Flanders, William Daniels, Mark Harmon & Denzel Washington?
4. What is the oldest of the five 'classic' horse races?
5. At which hospital was "Doctor in the House" set?
6. Which rugby league team were the first winners of the Super League?
7. The Mississippi and Missouri rivers meet near to which major American city?
8. Which was the only Scottish club to win the Texaco Cup?
9. On which island did Napoleon die?
10. What is the capital of Jersey?

ANSWERS:

1. St Petersburg
2. St Peter
3. St Elsewhere
4. St Leger
5. St Swithin's
6. St Helens
7. St Louis
8. St Mirren
9. St Helena
10. St Helier

GAME SHOWS

1. Who was the presenter of "The Price is Right" in the 1980's?

2. Which TV show was the subject of the programme "Cuddly Toys & Conveyor Belts"?

3. In which game show would you play 'Double Money' and 'Big Money'?

4. Who is the host on "Eggheads"?

5. Which show was introduced with the line, "From Norwich, it's the quiz of the week"?

6. Which game show links Paul Daniels and Bob Monkhouse as presenters?

7. Who was the original presenter of "You Bet!"?

8. Alan Taylor, Derek Batey and Julian Clary have all compered which TV game show?

9. Which TV game show featured Dusty Bin?

10. Whose catchphrases included "super, smashing, great" and "look at what you could have won"?

ANSWERS:

1. Leslie Crowther

2. "The Generation Game"

3. "Family Fortunes"

4. Dermot Murnaghan

5. "Sale of the Century"

6. "Wipeout"

7. Bruce Forsyth

8. "Mr & Mrs"

9. "3-2-1"

10. Jim Bowen

TAKE A CHANCE 41

In this round each correct answer is worth 2 points making a possible score of 20. However if you get any question wrong your score for this round is halved. If you are not sure, leave an answer blank and you still score 2 points for each correct answer (unless you get one wrong!). There is a theme to the answers; if you get the theme early it will help with the other answers.

1. Which song did the Rolling Stones take to No 1 in May 1968?

2. What was the first novel by Tom Wolfe that was published in 1987?

3. Every year in early July in Tarragona, there is a competition between 6 international manufacturers of what?

4. Played by Richard Armitage in the BBC series "Robin Hood", who is the Sheriff of Nottingham's second in command?

5. What device is fitted to the spout a hand pump to help give beer a he?

6. Which 1978 Elton John No 4 hit was a tribute to a Rocket Records motorcycle courier killed in a road accident?

7. Atlas, Delta, Redstone and Titan are names of what developed by the USA

8. Who led the 'Dambusters' squadron on its most famous mission?

9. What is the informal name that can be used for an old car or a sausage?

10. Which children's TV character works in Pontypandy?

ANSWERS:

1. "Jumping Jack Flash"
2. "The Bonfire of the Vanities"
3. Fireworks
4. Sir Guy of Gisbourne
5. Sparkler
6. "Song for Guy"
7. Rockets
8. Wing Commander Guy Gibson
9. Banger
10. Fireman Sam

POT LUCK 42

1. After which famous actor are the Society of London Theatre Awards named?

2. What do we call the food that Americans call jelly?

3. Which city state came into existence in 1929, after a treaty between Mussolini and the Pope?

4. What was the profession of Nell Gwynne before she became Charles the II's mistress?

5. What is the name of the stately home in Northamptonshire owned by the Spencer family?

6. Simba is the Swahili word for which animal?

7. Which country was annexed by China in 1950?

8. In the UK, which animal's hair was traditionally used to make shaving brushes?

9. Which country is Paddington Bear from?

10. Which country invaded the Falkland Islands on 2nd April 1982?

ANSWERS:

1. Sir Laurence Olivier

2. Jam

3. Vatican City

4. Actress

5. Althorp

6. Lion

7. Tibet

8. Badger

9. Peru

10. Argentina

FILM HEROES

1. Which actor starred in the "Superman" films of the 70's & 80's?

2. What was Dirty Harry's surname?

3. Who was the star of the "Naked Gun" films?

4. Which actor starred in the 1985 film "Commando"?

5. In which film did Kevin Costner play Union soldier Lieutenant John Dunbar?

6. Which character is played by Harrison Ford in "Patriot Games" and "Clear and Present Danger"?

7. Martin Riggs and Roger Murtagh are the central characters in which series of films?

8. What was Rambo's first name?

9. Which film hero married Tracy Draco?

10. Which actor played Batman in the 2005 film "Batman Begins"?

ANSWERS:

1. Christopher Reeve

2. Callahan

3. Leslie Nielsen

4. Arnold Schwarzenegger

5. "Dances With Wolves"

6. Jack Ryan

7. "Lethal Weapon"

8. John

9. James Bond (in OHMSS)

10. Christian Bale

LITERATURE

1. Which prolific British romantic author wrote the novel "Virgin in Paris" in 1968?

2. Flora Poste is the central character in which 1932 novel by Stella Gibbons?

3. Who is the head of the gang of thieves in "Oliver Twist"?

4. Who wrote the play "Twelfth Night"?

5. Heathcliff and Cathy are central characters in which famous novel"?

6. Which author created George Smiley?

7. Della Street was the secretary of which fictional lawyer?

8. Which female Irish author wrote "Evening Class" in 1996 and "Tara Road" in 1998?

9. In "Great Expectations", which character was jilted and still wore her wedding dress year's later?

10. Samuel Langhorne Clemens was the real name of which author?

ANSWERS:

1. Barbara Cartland

2. "Cold Comfort Farm"

3. Fagin

4. William Shakespeare

5. "Wuthering Heights"

6. John Le Carre

7. Perry Mason

8. Maeve Binchy

9. Miss Havisham

10. Mark Twain

SPORTING FIRSTS

1. Which American jockey was the first to win the Kentucky and Epsom Derbies?

2. At Nottingham in 1971, who became the first national hunt jockey to ride 1000 winners?

3. Who were the first English football team to win the European Cup?

4. Who was the first man to run a sub 4 minute mile?

5. Who was the first black player to captain the Great Britain Rugby League team?

6. Who was the first England Rugby Union player to win 100 caps?

7. Who became the first man to be ejected from a Grand Slam tennis tournament at the 1990 Australian Open?

8. In 1985, who became the first German golfer to win the US Masters?

9. Who was the first boxer to win the World Heavyweight Title on 3 occasions?

10. Who was the first cricketer to captain England in fifty test matches?

ANSWERS:

1. Steve Cauthen

2. Stan Mellor

3. Manchester United

4. Roger Bannister

5. Ellery Hanley

6. Jason Leonard (Vs France – Feb 2003)

7. John McEnroe

8. Bernhard Langer

9. Muhammad Ali (Cassius Clay)

10. Mike Atherton

TAKE A CHANCE 42

In this round each correct answer is worth 2 points making a possible score of 20. However if you get any question wrong your score for this round is halved. If you are not sure, leave an answer blank and you still score 2 points for each correct answer (unless you get one wrong!)

1. What colour are the majority of the seats in the new Wembley Stadium?

2. Who is the longest serving presenter in the history of "Blue Peter"?

3. Who stood trial for the murder of Ronald Goldman?

4. Who played the piano on the Wham! Hit "Edge of Heaven"?

5. Benjamin Briggs was the captain of which famous ship that lost its entire crew in the Atlantic Ocean in 1872?

6. "Courtesy and Care" is the motto of which motoring organisation?

7. In the film "The Adventures of Priscilla, Queen of the Desert" two drag queens perform a version of which Abba hit?

8. Which Englishman coached Australia's national soccer team in 1996?

9. In 1997, a statue of which actor was erected outside the Wallace Monument in Stirling?

10. Which female tennis player owned a car bearing the registration plate X CZECH?

ANSWERS:

1. Red
2. John Noakes (12 years 6 months)
3. OJ Simpson
4. Elton John
5. Marie Celeste
6. AA (Automobile Association)
7. "Mamma Mia"
8. Terry Venables
9. Mel Gibson
10. Martina Navratilova

POT LUCK 43

1. The Battle of Britain was fought between Britain and which other country?

2. Which famous Scottish explorer and missionary went in search of the source of the Nile in the 19th century?

3. What emblem was adopted in 1991 as a symbol of AIDS awareness?

4. The characters "Flopsy", "Mopsy" and "Cottontail" were created by which children's author?

5. The Iron Gates Gorge lies on which European river?

6. Which veteran Welsh singer has worked with New Model Army, Art of Noise and the Simpsons?

7. Was Cyrano de Bergerac a real or fictitious character?

8. Which Berkshire airbase was the centre of protests against the stationing of cruise missiles in the UK in 1981?

9. In which English county are the towns of Colchester and Chelmsford?

10. Which creature appeared in the titles of the TV comedy series 'One Foot in the Grave'?

ANSWERS:

1. Germany

2. David Livingstone

3. Red Ribbon

4. Beatrix Potter

5. Danube

6. Tom Jones

7. Real

8. Greenham Common

9. Essex

10. Tortoise

KIDS' STUFF 02 (Children In Need)

1. Who wrote the novel "Stuart Little"?

2. What is the name of Aladdin's monkey?

3. Billy Batson is the true identity of which superhero?

4. Krusty the Clown makes regular appearances in which TV show?

5. Who was the pilot of Thunderbird 1?

6. Who wrote the children's story "Charlie and the Great Glass Elevator"?

7. Which Disney movie is set around Pride Rock?

8. "If you go down to the woods today" is the opening line to which song?

9. Which canine cartoon character was assisted by Velma, Daphne, Freddy and Shaggy?

10. What type of fish is Nemo in the Disney Pixar film "Finding Nemo"?

ANSWERS:

1. E B White

2. Abu

3. Captain Marvel

4. "The Simpsons"

5. Scott Tracy

6. Roald Dahl

7. "The Lion King"

8. "The Teddy Bears' Picnic"

9. Scooby Doo

10. Clown Fish

THE USA (Thanksgiving)

1. Yellowstone Park is mainly situated within which US State?

2. The Texas State Fair is held annually in which city?

3. Which group of islands were previously called the Sandwich Islands?

4. Which city in California was founded in 1848 as Fort Sutter?

5. In which American city are the headquarters of UNICEF?

6. In which American city are the headquarters of Microsoft?

7. In which American city is Independence Hall?

8. In which state is the Pentagon?

9. CNN has its headquarters in which US city?

10. Which American city is nicknamed "The Crescent City"?

ANSWERS:

1. Wyoming

2. Dallas

3. Hawaii

4. Sacramento

5. New York

6. Seattle

7. Philadelphia

8. Virginia

9. Atlanta

10. New Orleans

THE B LIST

1. The NBA is the governing body of which sport in the United States?

2. Flesland Airport serves which Norwegian city?

3. Alan Ball began his career with which football club?

4. In Indian cookery, which appetiser consists of vegetables cooked in batter?

5. From which film did the band Duran Duran take their name?

6. A nomadic Arabic desert dweller is more commonly known as what?

7. Yeomen of the Guard are better known by what name?

8. The bossa nova originated in which country?

9. In cricket, what is the term for the crosspieces placed on top of the stumps?

10. Which musical instrument has parts called chanters and drones?

ANSWERS:

1. Basketball

2. Bergen

3. Blackpool

4. Bhajee

5. "Barbarella"

6. Bedouin

7. Beefeaters

8. Brazil

9. Bails

10. Bagpipes

TAKE A CHANCE 43

In this round each correct answer is worth 2 points making a possible score of 20. However if you get any question wrong your score for this round is halved. If you are not sure, leave an answer blank and you still score 2 points for each correct answer (unless you get one wrong!)

1. Which film star has been romantically linked with Sherilyn Fenn, Jennifer Grey, Winona Ryder and Kate Moss?

2. Which Nazi leader was tried for war crimes and crimes against humanity at Nuremberg in 1945 and 1946, was sentenced to death, but committed suicide hours before being executed?

3. Which song has been a No 2 hit for the Mindbenders and a No 1 hit for Phil Collins?

4. Which manager had a sign proclaiming 'This is Anfield' mounted on the wall above the exit from the player's tunnel at Liverpool's home ground?

5. Which Prime Minister once said, "The best argument against democracy is a 5 minute conversation with the average voter"?

6. Which South African city is sometimes referred to as 'The Mother City'?

7. What is the call sign of any of the US President's fleet of helicopters?

8. Which children's toy was originally called 'The Magic Screen'?

9. Which TV programme was presented by Stuart Hall and Eddie Waring?

10. In which film did Jack Nicholson play a personification of the devil called Daryl Van Horne?

ANSWERS:

1. Johnny Depp
2. Hermann Goering
3. "A Groovy Kind of Love"
4. Bill Shankly
5. Sir Winston Churchill
6. Cape Town
7. Marine One
8. Etch-A-Sketch
9. "It's A Knockout"
10. "The Witches of Eastwick"

POT LUCK 44

1. The triangle, bell and gong are all part of which family of instruments?

2. On which island off the coast of Wales would you find Beaumaris Castle?

3. In the Harry Potter books, the Hogwarts Express leaves from which London train station?

4. Which club won the last FA Cup final to be held under Wembley's Twin Towers?

5. Which former master of the Royal Mint appeared on the reverse of the old one pound note?

6. In which English county is the town of Gainsborough?

7. Caroline Aherne and Craig Cash created which TV family?

8. Which furry creatures picked up litter on Wimbledon Common?

9. An octet is a musical composition for how many instruments?

10. Which city was the planned destination of RMS Titanic when she sank in 1912?

ANSWERS:

1. Percussion

2. Anglesey

3. King's Cross

4. Chelsea

5. Sir Isaac Newton

6. Lincolnshire

7. "The Royle Family"

8. Wombles

9. 8

10. New York

QUOTATIONS

1. Which boxer said, "I float like a butterfly and sting like a bee"?

2. Which monarch said, "Let not poor Nelly starve"?

3. Which scientist said, "God does not play dice with the universe"?

4. Which US Secretary of State said, "Even a paranoid can have enemies"?

5. Which England manager famously said, "Do I not like that"?

6. Which US President said at his inauguration speech, "It is better to succeed with success than failure"?

7. Which tennis player told an umpire, "You are the pits" at Wimbledon in 1981?

8. Which British Prime Minister said, "A week is a long time in politics"?

9. Which famous playwright said, "Work is the curse of the drinking classes"?

10. Who said, "Gentlemen, include me out" in 1933 as he resigned from the Motion Picture Producers & Directors of America?

ANSWERS:

1. Muhammad Ali

2. Charles II

3. Albert Einstein

4. Dr Henry Kissinger

5. Graham Taylor

6. George W Bush

7. John McEnroe

8. Harold Wilson

9. Oscar Wilde

10. Sam Goldwyn

CHILDREN'S FILMS

1. Which 2001 film was advertised with the line "We scare because we care"?

2. Which actor starred in the 1999 film "Inspector Gadget"?

3. Which famous film features the Tin Man, the Scarecrow and the Cowardly Lion?

4. Which actor starred in the 1968 film "Chitty Chitty Bang Bang"?

5. Which 1998 animated film featured the voices of Woody Allen and Sylvester Stallone?

6. In which film does the central character search for the Great Pink Sea Snail?

7. Which actor played Eddie Valiant in the film "Who Framed Roger Rabbit"?

8. Which city is the setting for the 2007 Pixar film "Ratatouille"?

9. Kevin McCallister is the central character in which series of films?

10. Who provided the voice for Princess Fiona in the "Shrek" films?

ANSWERS:

1. "Monsters, Inc"

2. Matthew Broderick

3. "The Wizard of Oz"

4. Dick Van Dyke

5. "Antz"

6. "Doctor Dolittle"

7. Bob Hoskins

8. Paris

9. "Home Alone"

10. Cameron Diaz

BRITISH ISLES

1. Where in London is Nelson's Column?

2. Which park separates the football grounds of Liverpool and Everton?

3. Which Cheshire town is the site of a major railway junction?

4. In which county is Ironbridge Gorge?

5. At which racecourse is the Oaks run?

6. In which county are Plymouth and Torquay?

7. Manchester is situated on which river?

8. Which Scottish city is known as the "Capital of the Highlands"?

9. Which royal residence on the Isle of Wight was built for Queen Victoria in 1845?

10. What is the seat of the Duke of Bedford?

ANSWERS:

1. Trafalgar Square

2. Stanley Park

3. Crewe

4. Shropshire

5. Epsom

6. Devon

7. Irwell

8. Inverness

9. Osborne House

10. Woburn Abbey

TAKE A CHANCE 44

In this round each correct answer is worth 2 points making a possible score of 20. However if you get any question wrong your score for this round is halved. If you are not sure, leave an answer blank and you still score 2 points for each correct answer (unless you get one wrong!)

1. Which actor starred in the 1999 film "The Sixth Sense"?

2. The adjective renal refers to which part of the body?

3. "Quality food, honestly priced" is the slogan of which supermarket chain?

4. Which Welsh snooker player won the World Championship at his first attempt in 1979?

5. Smedley the Dog is the arch enemy of which animated penguin?

6. The 'Bada-Bing' was a fictional go-go bar featured in which television series?

7. Who was the British Secretary of State for War whose portrait featured on the most famous recruitment poster of WWI?

8. Which Boomtown Rats No 1 featured the line, "It's only 8 o'clock but you're already bored"?

9. In which country was Oscar winning actress Charlize Theron born?

10. Which radio programme was introduced with the line, "Are you sitting comfortably, then I'll begin"?

ANSWERS:

1. Bruce Willis
2. Kidneys
3. Waitrose
4. Terry Griffiths
5. Chilly Willy
6. "The Sopranos"
7. Lord Kitchener
8. "Rat Trap"
9. South Africa
10. "Listen with Mother"

DECEMBER

POT LUCK 45

1. In which Dorset town was the book and film 'The French Lieutenant's Woman' mainly set?

2. Which profession does the trade union the NASUWT represent?

3. Vocalist Alison Moyet and keyboard player Vince Clarke made up which duo?

4. Which British actor married his second wife Shakira Baksh a former Miss Guyana finalist in 1973?

5. First published in 1966, what colour was Chairman Mao's Little Book of Quotations?

6. Which infamous murderer went on a killing spree in London in 1888?

7. In which language is the Doomsday book written?

8. Prague is the capital of which country?

9. The cobnut and the filbert are other names for which nut?

10. Which American intelligence and counter-intelligence agency was established in 1947?

ANSWERS:

1. Lyme Regis

2. Teaching

3. Yazoo

4. Michael Caine

5. Red

6. Jack the Ripper

7. Latin

8. Czech Republic

9. Hazel Nut

10. CIA

FILM QUOTATIONS

Which films do the following quotes come from?

1. "I love the smell of napalm in the morning"

2. "Infamy, infamy, they've all got it in for me"

3. "Show me the money!"

4. "I'll have what she's having…"

5. "Hasta la vista baby"

6. "I do wish we could chat for longer, but I'm having an old friend for dinner"

7. "He's not the Messiah – he's a very naughty boy"

8. "Louis, I think this is the beginning of a beautiful friendship"

9. "Is it raining? I hadn't noticed"

10. "We want the finest wines available to humanity, we want them here and we want them now"

ANSWERS:

1. "Apocalypse Now"

2. "Carry On Cleo"

3. "Jerry Maguire"

4. "When Harry Met Sally"

5. "Terminator II"

6. "Silence of the Lambs"

7. "Life of Brian"

8. "Casablanca"

9. "Four Weddings and a Funeral"

10. "Withnail and I"

BRITISH HISTORY

1. Which monarch founded the Order of the British Empire, George III, IV, V or VI?

2. Who was Prime Minister when Queen Victoria died?

3. Who introduced the potato and tobacco into the British Isles?

4. Who was the Minister of Health who established the National Health Service?

5. Who famously said, "We are not amused"?

6. At which battle was King James IV of Scotland killed?

7. King Edward VIII renounced the throne to marry whom?

8. In which city did Diana, Princess of Wales die?

9. Who designed the Clifton Suspension bridge, which was completed in 1864, 5 years after his death?

10. Which monarch was supported by the Cavaliers during the English Civil War?

ANSWERS:

1. George V

2. Marquis of Salisbury

3. Sir Walter Raleigh

4. Aneurin Bevan

5. Queen Victoria

6. Battle of Flodden

7. Wallis Simpson

8. Paris

9. Isambard Kingdom Brunel

10. Charles I

MORE NUMBERS

1. How many dominoes are in a normal set?

2. At which number Rillington Place did murderer John Christie live?

3. What number is dos in Spanish?

4. How many sides does a trapezium have?

5. How many straight lines are there on a Football pitch?

6. How many yards in a mile?

7. A chessboard has how many squares?

8. How many of the United States are physically connected?

9. How many episodes of "Fawlty Towers" have there been?

10. How many strings does a Spanish Guitar have?

ANSWERS:

1. 28

2. 10

3. 2

4. 4

5. 17

6. 1760

7. 64

8. 48

9. 12

10. 6

TAKE A CHANCE 45

In this round each correct answer is worth 2 points making a possible score of 20. However if you get any question wrong your score for this round is halved. If you are not sure, leave an answer blank and you still score 2 points for each correct answer (unless you get one wrong!)

1. Simon Le Bon is the singer with which pop group?

2. Who was the hunter who continually tried to catch Bugs Bunny?

3. Which country has approximately 20% of the world's population?

4. Which Italian won a Best Actress Oscar for her performance in the 1960 film "Two Women"?

5. Which politician and social reformer was nicknamed 'Lord Porn'?

6. Which Field Marshal was renowned for the military campaigns he waged on behalf of the German Army in North Africa during WWII?

7. "Land of Hope and Glory" could be heard after the closing credits of which sitcom?

8. Which manager gave Alan Shearer his first England cap?

9. Which piece of music is used as the Scottish national anthem at the Commonwealth Games?

10. Which 1970's chart-topping single is often played at discos where dancers spell out the four letters of the song's title with their arms?

ANSWERS:

1. Duran Duran

2. Elmer Fudd

3. China

4. Sophia Loren

5. Lord Longford

6. Erwin Rommel

7. "It Ain't Half Hot Mum"

8. Graham Taylor

9. "Scotland the Brave"

10. "YMCA"

POT LUCK 46

1. What kind of card is referred to as plastic money?

2. Which city is the capital of Japan?

3. Mount Olympus is the highest point on which Mediterranean island?

4. What was the name of the seventh Cavalry General who was killed at Little Bighorn?

5. Which country's National Anthem begins with the words 'Oh say, can you see'?

6. In which modern day country did Vlad the Impaler, who was the historical inspiration for Count Dracula, live?

7. What 'P' is the name of the currency in Colombia, Cuba and Chile?

8. Which film duo had an 'Excellent Adventure' and went on a 'Bogus Journey?

9. In which island group are Stronsay, Westray and Hoy?

10. In Boris Pasternak's novel which title character was in love with Lara Antipova?

ANSWERS:

1. Credit Card

2. Tokyo

3. Cyprus

4. George Armstrong Custer

5. USA

6. Romania

7. Peso

8. Bill & Ted

9. Orkney Islands

10. "Dr Zhivago"

COPS ON THE BOX

1. Who was the star of the TV series "Hawaii Five-0"?

2. Which police series starred John Thaw and Dennis Waterman?

3. In which TV series did James Ellis play Sergeant Bert Lynch?

4. In which TV series did Stephen Tompkinson and Nick Berry play detectives?

5. Mark Wingett played which character from 1984 to 2005 in "The Bill"?

6. What was the name of the San Francisco detective played by Raymond Burr?

7. Who played the animal loving detective Tom McCabe in the TV series "Badger"?

8. Which actor stars in "A Touch of Frost"?

9. Detective Sergeant Chisholm & Sergeant Rycott featured in which TV series?

10. Which detective worked for Chief Inspector Barney Crozier?

ANSWERS:

1. Jack Lord

2. "The Sweeney"

3. "Z-Cars"

4. "In Deep"

5. Jim Carver

6. Ironside

7. Jerome Flynn

8. David Jason

9. "Minder"

10. Jim Bergerac

FILM MUSIC

1. Meco had a top 10 hit in 1977 with the theme music for which film?

2. The song "Whistle While You Work" was featured in which Disney film?

3. "A Whole New World" by Peabo Bryson & Regina Belle was the theme song to which Disney film?

4. The song "My Favourite Things" was featured in which musical?

5. Who collaborated with Giorgio Moroder on the theme for "Electric Dreams"?

6. "Moon River" was the theme to which 1960's film?

7. Which British composer and performer recorded the musical soundtrack for the 1984 film "The Killing Fields"?

8. Who wrote the musical score for the film "Born Free"?

9. Who won an Oscar in 2000 for the song "You'll Be in My Heart"?

10. Which Bee Gees song featured in the opening sequence to the film "Saturday Night Fever"?

ANSWERS:

1. "Star Wars"

2. "Snow White & the Seven Dwarfs"

3. "Aladdin"

4. "The Sound of Music"

5. Phil Oakey

6. "Breakfast at Tiffany's"

7. Mike Oldfield

8. John Barry

9. Phil Collins

10. "Stayin' Alive"

ANOTHER A LIST

1. The Giant's Causeway is situated in which county in Northern Ireland?

2. Chris De Burgh was born in which South American country?

3. The 2nd and 6th Presidents of the USA were father and son, what was their surname?

4. What is the scientific study of the remains left by earlier peoples?

5. In "Dynasty" who was Fallon's mother?

6. The Costa del Sol is part of which region of Spain?

7. Which Belgian team has won both the European Cup Winner's Cup and the UEFA Cup?

8. Which 1997 Steven Spielberg film starred Morgan Freeman, Anthony Hopkins and Nigel Hawthorne and told of the mutiny on a 19th Century slave ship?

9. Which pop group had a No 1 single in 1998 with "Turn Back Time"?

10. What is the earliest known name for the island of Britain used by Greek geographers from the 4th century BC?

ANSWERS:

1. Antrim

2. Argentina

3. Adams

4. Archaeology

5. Alexis

6. Andalucia

7. Anderlecht

8. "Amistad"

9. Aqua

10. Albion

TAKE A CHANCE 46

In this round each correct answer is worth 2 points making a possible score of 20. However if you get any question wrong your score for this round is halved. If you are not sure, leave an answer blank and you still score 2 points for each correct answer (unless you get one wrong!)

1. Gary Lineker and David Gower were team captains on which sport quiz?

2. Which novelist created the character Harry Palmer?

3. Which pop singer is nicknamed 'Alf'?

4. Captain Bligh was the victim of a mutiny on which ship?

5. The River Nile flows into which sea?

6. What is Japan's tallest mountain?

7. Which was the first English League club to install a plastic pitch?

8. What colour is the liqueur crème de menthe?

9. Which 1970's film won Oscars for Best Picture, Best Actor, Best Actress, Best Director and Best Screenplay?

10. Which "On the Buses" star opened the first cash dispenser in Enfield in 1967?

ANSWERS:

1. "They Think It's All Over"

2. Len Deighton

3. Alison Moyet

4. HMS Bounty

5. Mediterranean

6. Mount Fuji

7. Queens Park Rangers

8. Green

9. "One Flew Over the Cuckoo's Nest"

10. Reg Varney

POT LUCK 47 (Christmas Trivia)

1. In which town was Jesus born?

2. The fifth Sunday before Christmas is traditionally known as 'Stir-Up Sunday'; what is stirred up?

3. How many ships did I see come sailing by on "Christmas Day in the morning"?

4. Which of the Goons wrote "I'm walking Backwards for Christmas"?

5. Which Christmas tradition was initiated by J C Horsley and Henry Cole in 1843?

6. What have the citizens of Oslo given to the citizens of London each Christmas since 1947?

7. According to the Christmas carol, which monarch looked out on the Feast of Stephen?

8. Which TV family has a dog called "Santa's Little Helper"?

9. Deglet Noor, often served at Christmas, is a popular Tunisian variety of which fruit?

10. Who is the patron saint of merchants, sailors, pawnbrokers, children and Russia?

ANSWERS:

1. Bethlehem

2. Christmas Pudding

3. 3

4. Spike Milligan

5. Sending Christmas Cards

6. Christmas Tree

7. King Wenceslas

8. "The Simpsons"

9. Date

10. Saint Nicholas

CHRISTMAS MUSIC

1. Which singer had a Christmas No. 1 in 1985 with "Merry Christmas Everyone"?

2. What was the title of Leona Lewis's 2006 Christmas No 1 song?

3. Which song begins, "Dashing through the snow, in a one-horse open sleigh"?

4. What was the title of Bob the Builder's 2000 Christmas No. 1?

5. According to the Christmas song, how many lords-a-leaping were there?

6. Which group were "Lonely This Christmas" at the top of the charts in 1974?

7. Who wrote the song "White Christmas"?

8. What was the title of Michael Jackson's only Christmas No. 1 in 1995?

9. Which group had their 3rd consecutive Christmas No. 1 single in 1998?

10. Which group had a top ten hit in 1973 with "I Wish it Could Be Christmas Every Day"?

ANSWERS:

1. Shakin' Stevens

2. "A Moment Like This"

3. "Jingle Bells"

4. "Can We Fix It"

5. 10

6. Mud

7. Irving Berlin

8. "Earth Song"

9. Spice Girls

10. Wizzard

CHRISTMAS INITIAL SUCCESS

The first letter of each answer to questions 1 – 9 spells out the name of something associated with Christmas. Question 10 relates to that.

1. What is a traditional Christmas indoor plant that is said to be named after a US diplomat?

2. Which religious season includes the 4 Sundays before Christmas?

3. Who was born on Christmas Day 1923 and played Meg Richardson in "Crossroads"?

4. According to the words of the children's song, "All I want for Christmas is my two front ..." what?

5. Which English ruler banned Christmas carols and festivities between 1649 and 1660?

6. In 'The Twelve Days of Christmas' song, what were the maids doing?

7. In which ocean is the Australian territory of Christmas Island?

8. Which parasitic plant associated with Christmas is called 'Herbe de la Croix' in France?

9. What is the Christian festival that marks the end of the Christmas festivities?

10. In Britain, the most popular version of this is based on which fairy tale?

ANSWERS:

1. Poinsettia
2. Advent
3. Noele Gordon
4. Teeth
5. Oliver Cromwell
6. Milking
7. Indian
8. Mistletoe
9. Epiphany
10. "Cinderella"

CHRISTMAS AT THE MOVIES

1. Who played The Grinch in the 2000 film "How the Grinch Stole Christmas"??

2. Which star of silent movies died on Christmas Day 1977?

3. In the 1996 film "Jingle All the Way", what was the name of the toy that Arnold Schwarzenegger tries to get for his son on Christmas Eve?

4. Who played Kris Kringle in the 1994 version of "Miracle on 34th Street"?

5. In which 2003 film is the central character named after the disposable nappy that he was wearing at the start of the film?

6. During which war is the 1983 film "Merry Christmas, Mr Lawrence" set?

7. Which Tim Burton movie has been re-released in 3-D for Christmas 2006?

8. Who played dancer Ted Hanover in the 1942 classic "Holiday Inn"?

9. Which 1993 film starred Billy Bob Thornton as a conman?

10. In the classic "It's A Wonderful Life", what was the name of George Bailey's guardian angel?

ANSWERS:

1. Jim Carrey
2. Charlie Chaplin
3. Turbo Man
4. Richard Attenborough
5. "Elf"
6. WWII
7. "The Nightmare Before Christmas"
8. Fred Astaire
9. "Bad Santa"
10. Clarence

TAKE A CHANCE 47 (Christmas)

In this round each correct answer is worth 2 points making a possible score of 20. However if you get any question wrong your score for this round is halved. If you are not sure, leave an answer blank and you still score 2 points for each correct answer (unless you get one wrong!)

1. Who appeared as Scrooge's nephew in the 1983 film 'Mickey's Christmas Carol'?

2. If you were born on Christmas Day, what would your star-sign be?

3. The world's largest Christmas cracker was made (and pulled) in which country in 2001?

4. What game did British and German soldiers famously play during the Christmas Day truce in 1914?

5. Which parasitic plant was sacred to the Druids?

6. 'Meleagris gallopavo' is the Latin name for which part of the Christmas dinner?

7. Which 1982 Christmas hit by David Essex shared its title with a Shakespeare play?

8. Which well-known Christmas items were marketed in the 1850s under the name of Smith's Bon Bons?

9. Who was the first Holy Roman Emperor, crowned in Rome on Christmas Day 800 AD?

10. Which Christmas carol do you associate with Ilex Aquifolium and Hedera Helix?

ANSWERS:

1. Donald Duck
2. Capricorn
3. UK (at Saracen's Rugby Club)
4. Football
5. Mistletoe
6. Turkey
7. "A Winter's Tale"
8. Christmas Crackers
9. Charlemagne
10. "The Holly and the Ivy"

POT LUCK 48

1. Which trio wrote and produced hits for Jason Donovan and Rick Astley?

2. Alaska is the largest of the 50 US states, which is the second largest?

3. What is the term for holy war undertaken by Muslims?

4. The Isle of Man is situated in which sea?

5. According to the Elton John song, who was "Travelling tonight on a plane"?

6. Famous for pottery, which Dutch town is the birthplace of artist Jan Vermeer?

7. In which country is the source of the River Rhine?

8. Although he was born in Watford, which of 'The Goons' was the grandson of the Vice-President of Peru?

9. What is the name given to the upper stretches of to the River Thames above Oxford?

10. Which island lies in the Bay of Naples?

ANSWERS:

1. Stock, Aitken & Waterman

2. Texas

3. Jihad

4. Irish Sea

5. Daniel

6. Delft

7. Switzerland

8. Michael Bentine

9. Isis

10. Capri

TUTTI FRUTTI

1. Who was the lead singer with the 90's band Black Grape?

2. Formerly called Orange Free State, now simply Free State, is a province of which country?

3. Which female singer was the first signing to the Beatles' Apple label?

4. Who directed and starred in the 1971 film "Bananas"?

5. Which American singer had a hit with "Blueberry Hill"?

6. Which Russian wrote the play "The Cherry Orchard" in 1904?

7. Who wrote "James and the Giant Peach"?

8. Which duo had a hit in 1990 with "Strawberry Fields Forever"?

9. Harry Lime is the central character in which novel?

10. The Phantom Raspberry Blower of Old London Town featured in which TV show?

ANSWERS:

1. Shaun Ryder

2. South Africa

3. Mary Hopkin

4. Woody Allen

5. Fats Domino

6. Anton Chekhov

7. Roald Dahl

8. Candy Flip

9. "The Third Man"

10. "The Two Ronnies"

FILM TRIBUTES

1. Which actor played Jim Morrison in "The Doors"?

2. Who was the subject of the multi Oscar winning 2004 film "The Aviator"?

3. Which artist was the subject of the film "Lust for Life"?

4. Which actor played Lenny Bruce in the 1974 biopic "Lenny"?

5. Which comedian was the subject of the 1999 film "Man on the Moon"?

6. Ben Kingsley won a best actor Oscar in 1982 for his performance in which film?

7. The 1990 film "Postcards from the Edge" was based on the life of which actress?

8. Who played Tina Turner in the film "What's Love Got to Do With It"?

9. Who played Bobby Darin in the 2004 biopic "Beyond the Sea"?

10. Which 1995 film tells the story of rebel Scottish leader William Wallace?

ANSWERS:

1. Val Kilmer

2. Howard Hughes

3. Vincent Van Gogh

4. Dustin Hoffman

5. Andy Kaufman

6. "Gandhi"

7. Carrie Fisher

8. Angela Bassett

9. Denzel Washington

10. "Braveheart"

KINGS & QUEENS

1. The song "The King of the Swingers" is featured in which musical film?

2. Which Australian state is named after a British Queen?

3. Which country was the setting for the film "The King & I"?

4. Who wrote the comic novel "The Queen & I" in 1993?

5. Which sport is known as "The Sport of Kings"?

6. Who played the title role in the 1971 film "Mary, Queen of Scots"?

7. The father of the title character in which Shakespeare play is the King of Denmark?

8. What was the title of Queen's first British No 1 single?

9. Which Scot once said, "Jimmy Hill is to football what King Herod was to babysitting"?

10. Which singer is known as 'The Queen of Soul'?

ANSWERS:

1. "The Jungle Book"

2. Victoria

3. Siam (Thailand)

4. Sue Townsend

5. Horse Racing

6. Vanessa Redgrave

7. Hamlet

8. "Bohemian Rhapsody"

9. Tommy Docherty

10. Aretha Franklin

TAKE A CHANCE 48 (The Last Round)

In this round each correct answer is worth 2 points making a possible score of 20. However if you get any question wrong your score for this round is halved. If you are not sure, leave an answer blank and you still score 2 points for each correct answer (unless you get one wrong!)

1. Who was the last Chancellor of West Germany?

2. What is the last book of the New Testament?

3. What was the title of the last Bruce Lee film to be completed before his death?

4. Who was the last of Henry VIII's wives?

5. "Super Trouper" was which group's last number one single?

6. How many singles matches are played on the last day of the Ryder Cup?

7. What was the last of the "Dirty Harry" films?

8. Gary Lineker made his last international appearance against which country?

9. What is the last letter of the Greek alphabet?

10. Which play recounts the last hours of Willy Loman?

ANSWERS:

1. Helmut Kohl

2. Revelation

3. "Enter the Dragon"

4. Catherine Parr

5. Abba

6. 12

7. "The Dead Pool"

8. Sweden

9. Omega

10. "Death of a Salesman"

BONUS QUIZZES

POT LUCK 49

1. Which musical told the tale of an English governess who travels to Siam to teach the king's children?

2. BS are the initial letters in the post codes of which city?

3. In the early 1960's who was the owner of the Carousel Club in Dallas?

4. Which golfer won the 1997 US Masters by 12 strokes?

5. Moussaka is a traditional dish from which country?

6. Which gold medal winning boxer lit the Olympic flame at the Atlanta games in 1996?

7. In which US state were Jimmy Carter and Martin Luther King born?

8. Which mountain range in South America extends through 7 different countries?

9. What was the name of the Ewings' home in "Dallas"?

10. Which German group recorded the official theme to the Tour de France in 1983?

ANSWERS:

1. "The King and I"

2. Bristol

3. Jack Ruby

4. Tiger Woods

5. Greece

6. Muhammad Ali

7. Georgia

8. Andes

9. Southfork

10. Kraftwerk

MORE G-MEN

1. Which South African won his second US Open Golf Championship title in 2004?

2. Who succeeded Konstantin Chernenko as Secretary General of the Soviet Communist Party?

3. Which actor played Tony Soprano in "The Sopranos"?

4. Who played D I Dave Creegan in the 3 TV series of "Touching Evil" in the late 1990's

5. Which Hollywood actor won his only Oscar for the 1934 film "It Happened One Night"?

6. Which influential economist was appointed Chairman of the US Federal Reserve Board in 1987?

7. Which singer's first UK No 1 was "Unchained Melody" in 2002?

8. Who, in 1990, scored the most runs by one batsman in a Test Match?

9. Which author created and has written 23 novels featuring the antique dealing character "Lovejoy"?

10. Who won a Best Supporting Actor Oscar in 1996 for his role in the film "Jerry Maguire"?

ANSWERS:

1. Reteif Goosen

2. Mikhail Gorbachev

3. James Gandolfini

4. Robson Green

5. Clark Gable

6. Alan Greenspan

7. Gareth Gates

8. Graham Gooch

9. Jonathan Gash

10. Cuba Gooding JR

ANIMAL KINGDOM

1. Cocker, Springer and King Charles are all breeds of which dog?

2. What type of creature is a crane?

3. The first cats known to have been domesticated came from which country?

4. Which black and white whale is also known as a grampus?

5. Sucker-footed, hog-nosed and leaf-chinned are all types of what mammal?

6. What name is given to the study of insects?

7. What is the collective term for a group of geese not in flight?

8. What is the name given to the long hair found on the head and shoulders of a male lion?

9. What large wading bird, with a long neck, is said to deliver new-born babies?

10. How many legs does a millipede usually have in each segment of its body?

ANSWERS:

1. Spaniel

2. Bird

3. Egypt

4. Killer Whale

5. Bat

6. Entomology

7. Gaggle

8. Mane

9. Stork

10. Four

COUNTRIES

1. Ryanair is an international airline based in which European country?

2. In South America, the River Plate lies between Argentina and which other country?

3. The city of Gdansk is a major port in which European country?

4. The winter sports centre of Sapporo, the site of the 1972 Winter Olympics, is in which Asian country?

5. The Beqaa is a fertile valley in which middle-eastern country?

6. Finland was part of which country between 1809 and 1917?

7. Alberta and Manitoba are provinces of which country?

8. Hekla is an active volcano in which island country in the North Atlantic?

9. With which country does China share its longest land border?

10. In 1861, Victor Emmanuel II was proclaimed king of which newly-created European kingdom?

ANSWERS:

1. Republic of Ireland

2. Uruguay

3. Poland

4. Japan

5. Lebanon

6. Russia

7. Canada

8. Iceland

9. Mongolia

10. Italy

TAKE A CHANCE 49

In this round each correct answer is worth 2 points making a possible score of 20. However if you get any question wrong your score for this round is halved. If you are not sure, leave an answer blank and you still score 2 points for each correct answer (unless you get one wrong!)

1. Which David Bowie hit ends with the line, "Planet Earth is blue and there's nothing I can do"?

2. Buckingham Palace is situated at the end of which London street that leads to Nelson's Column?

3. In which James Bond film did Britt Ekland play Mary Goodnight?

4. Which singer was elected Mayor of Palm Springs, California in April 1988?

5. Who was the President of the United States when the Great Depression began in 1929?

6. The Borchester Echo is the newspaper featured in which radio series?

7. There are statues of Christopher Columbus, Ludwig van Beethoven and Duke Ellington in which New York park?

8. Which striker is the only player to have won 3 Football Writers' Footballer of the Year awards?

9. Maureen Bullock had a crush on her teacher Bernard Hedges in which classic sitcom?

10. Which was the last country to host the Summer and Winter Olympics in the same year?

ANSWERS:

1. "Space Oddity"
2. The Mall
3. "The Man with the Golden Gun"
4. Sonny Bono
5. Herbert Hoover
6. "The Archers"
7. Central Park
8. Thierry Henry
9. "Please Sir!"
10. Germany (1936 Berlin & Garmisch-Partenkirchen)

POT LUCK 50

1. The song "Any Dream Will Do" comes from which Andrew Lloyd Webber musical?

2. Where in the body is the hippocampus?

3. Who wrote the poem "To a Skylark", which begins with the line "Hail to thee, blithe spirit!"?

4. The bald eagle is the national bird of which country?

5. Which execution device was adopted as the standard form of capital punishment in France during the Revolution?

6. In pre-decimal currency, how many pennies were there in a shilling?

7. The Order of the Elephant is a high honour in which European country?

8. Which actress provided Jessica Rabbit's speaking voice in the film 'Who Framed Roger Rabbit?

9. Which country won the Battle of Agincourt in 1415?

10. What do the initials A.T.M. stand for?

ANSWERS:

1. "Joseph & the Amazing Technicolor Dreamcoat"

2. Brain

3. Shelly

4. USA

5. Guillotine

6. 12

7. Denmark

8. Kathleen Turner

9. England

10. Automated Teller Machine

MORE FAMOUS PEOPLE

1. Whose 1988 autobiography was entitled "Moonwalk"?

2. Who in 1985 became the youngest ever winner of the Wimbledon Men's Singles title?

3. Whose 1994 single "Take a Bow" ended her run of 33 consecutive top 10 hits?

4. Who wrote the novels "Fever Pitch" and "About A Boy"?

5. Which actor directed the 2004 Oscar winning film "Million Dollar Baby"?

6. Who in 1998 became the oldest man in space at the age of 77?

7. Who wrote the musical "On the Town"?

8. Which rugby union player was appointed England captain in 1988 at the age of 22?

9. Who became leader of the Labour Party in 1983?

10. Robert Zimmerman is the real name of which singer?

ANSWERS:

1. Michael Jackson

2. Boris Becker

3. Madonna

4. Nick Hornby

5. Clint Eastwood

6. John Glenn

7. Leonard Bernstein

8. Will Carling

9. Neil Kinnock

10. Bob Dylan

NUMBERS AGAIN

1. Which number can be found bottom centre of a darts board?

2. According to the title of their TV programme, at which number do the Kumars host their chat show?

3. How many inches are there in two feet?

4. According to tradition, how many years of bad luck does breaking a mirror bring?

5. What is the U.K telephone dialling code for Edinburgh?

6. At what age are children legally allowed to undertake paid work in the UK?

7. What is the minimum number of metals needed to form an alloy?

8. How many players are there in a volleyball team?

9. What is the minimum age for joining the French Foreign Legion?

10. New York City is divided into how many boroughs?

ANSWERS:

1. 3
2. 42
3. 24
4. 7
5. 0131
6. 13
7. 2
8. 6
9. 17
10. 5

RAINBOW

1. In motor racing, what colour flag is usually used to stop a race before the finish?

2. The flowers of which citrus tree are traditionally worn by a bride?

3. What colour are the petals of the flower known as the black-eyed susan?

4. A ski run specifically suited to beginners is marked by which colour?

5. What colour is the background of a motorway direction sign?

6. In the Ancient Mayan civilisation, which colour was recognised for its soothing effect on pregnant women and their unborn children?

7. To which group of flowers does the pansy belong?

8. Which colour ball in snooker is worth 3 points?

9. In the 'Mr. Men' books, what colour is Mr Bump beneath his bandages?

10. In the children's TV programme 'Rainbow', what colour was George the Hippo?

ANSWERS:

1. Red
2. Orange
3. Yellow
4. Green
5. Blue
6. Indigo
7. Violet
8. Green
9. Blue
10. Pink

TAKE A CHANCE 50

In this round each correct answer is worth 2 points making a possible score of 20. However if you get any question wrong your score for this round is halved. If you are not sure, leave an answer blank and you still score 2 points for each correct answer (unless you get one wrong!)

1. Which TV star has been married to Penny Dixon and actresses Patricia Maynard and Rula Lenska?

2. Which female writer was found murdered in Kenya in 1985?

3. Which group had hit albums called "Ocean Drive" and "Postcards from Heaven"?

4. What is the entrance to the Tower of London from the River Thames known as?

5. In which TV series did David Jason play the owner of the Jupiter Foundry?

6. What is the world's largest package delivery company, delivering more than 14 million packages per day to over 200 countries around the world?

7. Who became manager of Crystal Palace for the 4th time in 1999?

8. For his 90th birthday present, Plymouth Argyle registered which former Labour leader as a player and gave him the shirt number 90?

9. Which author was portrayed by Johnny Depp in the film "Finding Neverland"?

10. Which broadsheet was the first British newspaper to print a sudoku puzzle?

ANSWERS:

1. Dennis Waterman
2. Joy Adamson
3. Lighthouse Family
4. Traitor's Gate
5. "A Bit of a Do"
6. UPS (United Parcel Service)
7. Steve Coppell
8. Michael Foot
9. JM Barrie
10. Daily Telegraph

POT LUCK 51

1. Which country is the home of the Magyar people?

2. Wyatt Earp became an assistant marshal in which famous lawless frontier town?

3. What is the name given to the process of searching for gold using a circular dish in a stream of water?

4. What type of musical instrument sometimes has snares attached to it?

5. In which Scottish city does the Royal Mile run between the castle and Holyrood House?

6. Who wrote the 1974 novel 'Tinker, Tailor, Soldier, Spy'?

7. Doris Day's UK hit single 'Secret Love' came from which film?

8. Before decimalisation, what was the name of the large British coin that had a value of two shillings and sixpence?

9. Around what type of tree, in Sherwood Forest, did Robin Hood reputedly gather his merry men?

10. In the books by Leslie Charteris, what was the Saint's real name?

ANSWERS:

1. Hungary

2. Dodge City

3. Panning

4. Drums

5. Edinburgh

6. John Le Carre

7. "Calamity Jane"

8. Half Crown

9. Oak

10. Simon Templar

THE SUN AND THE MOON

1. Which singer duetted with Elton John on "Don't Let The Sun Go Down On Me" at Live Aid?

2. Who wrote the novel "The Moon and Sixpence"?

3. Who was the Roman god of the sun?

4. Which group had a No 1 hit in the 1970's with "Under the Moon of Love"?

5. Which country is nicknamed 'The Land of the Rising Sun'?

6. Who sang the song "Moon River" in the film "Breakfast at Tiffany's"?

7. Which TV series is set at Sun Hill?

8. What is Jupiter's largest moon?

9. Which sport is played by the Phoenix Suns?

10. Keith Moon was the drummer with which rock band?

ANSWERS:

1. George Michael

2. William Somerset Maugham

3. Apollo

4. Showaddywaddy

5. Japan

6. Audrey Hepburn

7. "The Bill"

8. Ganymede

9. Basketball

10. The Who

ART

1. What nationality was Pablo Picasso?

2. Who provided the vocals on the Art of Noise's 1988 Top 10 hit "Kiss"?

3. Which country claims ownership of the Elgin Marbles?

4. Which writer's only novel was "The Picture of Dorian Grey"?

5. What was George Stubbs most famous for painting?

6. Who played Ulysses Everett McGill in the 2000 film "O Brother Where Art Thou"?

7. Which late 19th Century French artist painted "Le Moulin Rouge"?

8. In which Italian city is the Uffizi Gallery?

9. What nationality was the celebrated sculptor Henry Moore?

10. How many paintings did Vicent van Gogh sell during his lifetime?

ANSWERS:

1. Spanish

2. Tom Jones

3. Greece

4. Oscar Wilde

5. Horses

6. George Clooney

7. Henri de Toulouse-Lautrec

8. Florence

9. British

10. One (for 400 francs)

SCIENCE

1. Who wrote the best selling book "A Brief History of Time" in 1988?

2. Which element comes first in the Periodic Table?

3. Who played the "perfect" woman Lisa, created by two nerdish boys, in the 1985 film Weird Science?

4. Which contains the most bones – the human arm or the human leg? *(Note: -the arm includes the hand and the leg includes the foot)*

5. Which all girl group had a Top 20 hit with "Chemistry" in 1981?

6. What is the more common name for poly methyl methacrylate?

7. Which Science Fiction author is credited with inventing the communications satellite?

8. Which of these is the odd one out – Angstrom, Chain, Light-Year, Second?

9. True or false – The scientific unit the Calorie was named after 18th Century French scientist Pierre de Calorie.

10. Who presented "Local Heroes", "What the Romans Did For Us" and "Tomorrows World"?

ANSWERS:

1. Stephen Hawking

2. Hydrogen

3. Kelly Le Brock

4. Arm – 30 (Leg – 29)

5. The Nolans

6. Perspex

7. Arthur C Clarke

8. Second (all the others are a measure of length)

9. False

10. Adam Hart-Davis

TAKE A CHANCE 51

In this round each correct answer is worth 2 points making a possible score of 20. However if you get any question wrong your score for this round is halved. If you are not sure, leave an answer blank and you still score 2 points for each correct answer (unless you get one wrong!)

1. Which piece of cloth, believed to bear an imprint of Christ's face, was denounced as a fake in 1988?

2. Which TV series featured the characters Superintendent Norman Mullett and DS George Toolan?

3. The Bromley Contingent were a group of followers of which punk band?

4. Which former Chelsea defender was nicknamed 'Chopper'?

5. Which sailor was the first cartoon character to have a statue erected in his honour?

6. In a TV advert, which footballer proclaimed, "I feel like chicken tonight"?

7. Which actor starred in the Razzie Award winning 2006 film "R V – Runaway Vacation"?

8. Which is the only country that has a coastline on the Atlantic and Indian Oceans?

9. Who wrote the novel "Wuthering Heights"?

10. Which comedian uses the catchphrases, "Time-waster!" and "Is your dad proud of you, son"?

ANSWERS:

1. Turin Shroud
2. "A Touch of Frost"
3. Sex Pistols
4. Ron Harris
5. Popeye
6. Ian Wright
7. Robin Williams
8. South Africa
9. Emily Bronte
10. Al Murray (The Pub Landlord)

POT LUCK 52

1. What do the letters M.A. stand for after a graduate's name?

2. On which famous London street does the British Prime Minister live?

3. With what form of entertainment was the American P.T. Barnum most associated?

4. What colour is Kermit the Frog?

5. In what country would you be if you were in Havana?

6. Which is the largest planet in the Solar System?

7. How many wings does a bee have?

8. In which country did the Boxer Uprising take place from 1899 to 1900?

9. Which cartoon bear first appeared in a British newspaper on the eighth of November 1920?

10. Under what pseudonym did children's author George Remi write the "Tintin" books?

ANSWERS:

1. Master of Arts

2. Downing Street

3. Circus

4. Green

5. Cuba

6. Jupiter

7. 4

8. China

9. Rupert

10. Hergé

POP MUSIC – THE No 1's

1. Which sex god reached No 1 with "You're The First, The Last, My Everything""

2. "Livin' La Vida Loca" was a 1999 No 1 for which singer?

3. Which movie tune stayed at No 1 in the UK charts for 15 weeks in 1994?

4. "In the Summertime" was a summer smash hit in 1970 for which band?

5. What follows this line from a 1979 UK No 1, "Giant steps are what you take"?

6. "There Must Be an Angel" was the only UK No 1 hit for which band?

7. What was Britney Spears debut single that shot to No 1 in 1999?

8. Which ex Spice Girl had a No 1 hit with "Lift Me Up"?

9. "I was working as a waitress in a cocktail bar" is a line from which 1981 No 1 hit?

10. Who had 3 reissued singles go to No 1 in 2005?

ANSWERS:

1. Barry White

2. Ricky Martin

3. "Love Is All Around"

4. Mungo Jerry

5. "Walking on the Moon"

6. Eurythmics

7. "Baby One More Time"

8. Geri Halliwell

9. "Don't You Want Me" – Human League

10. Elvis Presley

ART & LITERATURE

1. In which Russian city is the Hermitage Art Gallery?

2. Who wrote the novel "The Mill on the Floss"?

3. Which style of art was introduced by Pablo Picasso & Georges Braque in the early 20ᵗʰ Century?

4. Rhett Butler and Scarlett O'Hara first appeared in which novel?

5. What nationality was the abstract artist Jackson Pollack?

6. Who wrote the novel "Kane & Abel" in 1980?

7. Which artist painted "Swans Reflecting Elephants"?

8. Which American author uses the pseudonym Richard Bachman?

9. What is the former Palace of Kings in Paris that was converted into an art gallery by Napoleon in 1793?

10. Philip Pirrip is the central character of which Charles Dickens novel?

ANSWERS:

1. St Petersburg

2. George Eliot

3. Cubism

4. "Gone With The Wind"

5. American

6. Jeffrey Archer

7. Salvador Dali

8. Stephen King

9. The Louvre

10. "Great Expectations"

SPORTING FAMILIES

1. Who won most England Rugby caps, Rory or Tony Underwood?

2. What was the surname of New Zealand's international cricket playing brothers Dayle, Richard & Barry?

3. What was the surname of the British brothers who won an Olympic Gold medal in the Coxed Pairs in 1992?

4. Which of the Williams sisters was the first to win a Grand Slam singles title?

5. What is the name of Tony Greig's brother who played test cricket for England?

6. What was the surname of the brothers in England's 1966 World Cup winning team?

7. What nationality are rugby playing brothers Henry and Robbie Paul?

8. What is the name of Gavin Hastings' rugby union playing brother?

9. What was the surname of the 3 brothers who played in a 1st Division match for Southampton in October 1988?

10. Which of the Waugh brothers took most test match catches in their Australian careers?

ANSWERS:

1. Rory – 85 (Tony 29)

2. Hadlee

3. Searle

4. Serena (US Open 1999)

5. Ian

6. Charlton

7. New Zealanders

8. Scott

9. Wallace (Danny, Ray & Rod)

10. Mark – 181 (Steve 111)

TAKE A CHANCE 52

In this round each correct answer is worth 2 points making a possible score of 20. However if you get any question wrong your score for this round is halved. If you are not sure, leave an answer blank and you still score 2 points for each correct answer (unless you get one wrong!)

1. Which number can precede "letter word" and "minute warning"?

2. Which animal is the symbol of the Democratic Party in the USA?

3. In which 1961 film did Paul Newman play pool player 'Fast' Eddie Felson?

4. Who opened Britain's first family planning clinic in 1921?

5. At what age does a Jewish boy have his bar mitzvah?

6. Who was the first golfer to hold all 4 'Major' titles simultaneously?

7. Which Prime Minister granted a peerage to Marcia Williams?

8. What was the title of the Osmonds only UK No 1 hit single?

9. Featured in the "Dandy", what type of animal is Korky?

10. Which duo frequently assisted Police Commissioner Gordon and Police Chief O'Hara?

ANSWERS:

1. 4

2. Donkey

3. "The Hustler"

4. Marie Stopes

5. 13

6. Tiger Woods

7. Harold Wilson

8. "Love Me For a Reason"

9. Cat

10. Batman & Robin

Acknowledgements:

This book would not have been possible without the help of C A Solutions, Redtooth and the BBC People's Quiz who have all provided inspiration and questions for this volume. Thanks also to the quiz goers of The Bull's Head and Colebrook who have ensured that these questions are fully 'road tested'.